To Raise A Parent

A Path To Higher Consciousness

Jeremiah D. Kaynor
To Raise A Parent

Copyright © 2010 Jeremiah D. Kaynor

All rights reserved.

ISBN-13: 978-1470157838

ISBN-10: 1470157837

All rights reserved. Federal copyright law prohibits unauthorized reproduction by any means and imposes fines up to $25,000 for violations.

Jeremiah D. Kaynor
To Raise A Parent

In 2012, in the U.S. alone, 84% of men and 86% of women will become biological parents in their lives. 50% of marriages end in divorce with only 40% of the 2nd marriages surviving. 37% of families in the United States are successful blended families. Biological parents have their hands full, and most step-parents will tell you, their job is even more complicated. So with all the cards stacked against you, how do you come out alive? Better yet, how can you come out on top and not only learn how to be a parent, but a happier, more understanding, and more enlightened person? Well let's find out.

Jeremiah D. Kaynor
To Raise A Parent

Contents

The Beginning Of My Life ~ P.16
- The Beginning of Bonding ~ P.23

The Ego, The Mental "Complex" And The Pre-conceived Concepts ~ P.32
- True Self and the Ego ~ P.36
- The Complex ~ P.43
- Pre-conceived Concept ~ P.52
- My Troubling Ego ~ P.59
- Common Complexes and Egoic Actions ~ P.68

Faces Of The Ego: Jealousy, Control, And Identity ~ P.72
- The Face of Jealousy ~ P.73
- The Face of Identity ~ P.76
- Function VS. Identity ~ P.84
- The Face of Control ~ P.88

Letting Go ~ P.104
- Letting Go of Identity ~ P.108
- Letting Go of the Past ~ P.119
- Letting Go of Control ~ P.130
- Seeing What's Real ~ P.134

Breaking The Walls Of Pre-Conceived Concepts ~ P.140
- What We Are Taught ~ P.141
- What We Observe ~ P.144
- Opening Up The Mind ~ P.146

Being Unaware And Becoming Aware ~ P.150
- I Was Unaware and Blind ~ P.151
- Opening My Eyes and Mind ~ P.157
- Striving To Staying In The Present Moment ~ P.162
- Observing Your Emotions ~ P.165
- Giving Children Guidance From Your Higher Self ~ P.170

Parenting Partnership And Tips To Bring Ease On The Relationships ~ P.174
- A Co-Parenting Schedule ~ P.175
- The Ease of Boundaries ~ P.179
- Guidance From the Higher Self ~ P.184
- Working With Your Partner ~ P.187

Making Mistakes And Recovering From The Fall ~ P.192

The Archetype: The Step-Parent That Will Change The World ~ P.198

Jeremiah D. Kaynor
To Raise A Parent

Acknowledgment

I would like to thank my lovely wife for supporting me in this and for being a partner in the spiritual path of finding self, truth, and inner peace. She has been an inspiration and guiding light in my life. I have learned so much from her and can only pray that I can give back in life what she has given.

To my two beautiful children, I can't tell you how much I have learned about myself from having you in my life. I never imagined that love could be so powerful and so rewarding. They have both amazed me and I could never be able to tell them in words how proud I am of them. Never stop glowing, never stop shining, and never stop filling the world with beauty.

Thanks are also in order for Dr. Catherine Fox who has been an amazing guide and help through these years in helping me find my inner light. And I would like to thank my good friend Paul Cole for his amazingly natural insight into life and for the conversations that we have had as we both grew into the step-parenting role at the same time.

To Grace Rozon who has been a great help and very supportive. She has always been one of the kindest souls I have ever come across in life. Thank you for your help and unbiased opinions on my work. I truly value your thoughts. Also, to Carol Cory and Signe Feeney, thank you so much for taking the time to edit this book out of love and support. And Robert Michael Cory, thank you for believing in me and the book. Without all of you above, this would have never happened.

Finally, I would like to thank all of the men and women in the world that are taking on the role of being a step-parent. It is a beautiful gift, and when given from the true self, it can heal a thousand broken hearts. So let us move forward and learn how we can become the healers of these family units.

I would also like to mention that the teachings in this book are from experience and not from a certified doctor. In writing this book I understand that everyone's circumstances are different, but I hope what you read within these pages gives a little insight to the world you are experiencing now. The events described in this book are actual events. Names have been changed in order to protect anonymity where I felt it was important.

Jeremiah D. Kaynor
To Raise A Parent

If only I knew in the beginning what I know now, my children would have been able to transition better with someone that understood what they were experiencing. To Raise a Parent is my invitation to all step-parents-in-the-making to discover that this overlooked role contains magical spiritual transformation. Join me and shape-shift the world of these children that need our healing.

Become the healer.

11:11

Introduction

I have writing this book not just for you, the reader, but for myself as well. I started this book in the beginning of this wonderful adventure called parenthood, therefore, learning as I go, so you can see the progression in my life throughout the last four years.

When I started this book I was working toward taking the step into marriage and sealing the bond of "Family" forever with the ones I love. As I worked towards this dream, I was also raising a new part of me that fills specific roles in life; a partner, a friend, a parent, and a stepfather. I decided in the beginning of this path I have chosen, I would put down in words what I learn as I work towards being this person my stepchildren can look to for loving guidance; a true parent.

This book is an accumulation of the experience, lessons, and information I have discovered throughout my journey. The teachings I have left on these pages is not just to help you understand better what you and your dearest child are going through, but to be a guide for you on this path as well as into your heart and mind. It also will help ease the pain and confusion that COULD come with molding your life into these children's lives. My intention is to help you move more easily past possible road blocks in your new relationship and to give insight into your own thoughts and feelings that can arise.

I am a man that, when it comes to reading, does not have the longest attention span and, therefore I do not like long drawn out explanations about life. For that reason I feel it is not necessary to write down long-winded speeches on each subject you may have come across in other literature. I want to keep it to the point as much as possible. I want every teaching to be easy to understand, so it does not lose you in the moment. I have read and re-read many books and I don't want you to feel you have to go back just to understand the ideas in this book.

The teachings can help right away in your life so if there is any concept that I do repeat throughout my time with you, it is due to the importance of understanding the teaching.

The information in this book is vital to a relationship and gives needed insight to help that relationship grow into a strong bond of love and trust. This book will guide you to becoming the parent that can and will change the world of parenting. The book is not

JUST intended to make you a better parent or step-parent, but help you bloom into a full on, compassionate, understanding, loving, and inspiring parent as you gain a better understanding of yourself.

Unfortunately, most people, when finding themselves in these potentially magical relationships, feel thrown into the mix. You may feel like you jumped in and don't quite know how to swim yet. The words in this book will be a light in the dark that will give you insight into building a relationship with the one you love and the children they cherish. You too will come to grow closer than you have ever dreamed with these children that are now yours to love. As I grew and overcame the feelings of hurt, frustration, and confusion that came with this step-parenting relationship, I became better equipped to help you to understand the emotions you are going to encounter as you build your family. I can now share my life and understanding of what I learned. This has helped me learn about myself, my children, and to be able to direct and express my love clearly by guiding with a gentle hand, molding them properly, NOT into "well-adjusted", but well-loved and loving people, as I raise myself and grow into a loving stepfather and that is what I wish to help you become as well.

I will admit it is a confusing road. For me, the roller coaster of becoming a step-parent could never be more on edge or in the dark. Like a scary movie, it draws you into a comfortable spot only to unleash its terror on you when you least expect it.

One of the most amazing phenomenon's you will ever witness is the cutting words of a child. At an adult age where we could care less if someone says an unkind word to us or is a little mean, it will blow your mind how a child (mine age 9) can say something that cuts all the way to the bone. Then five minutes later they love you to death and everything is normal while you are left broken hearted and not sure why. Pain is deeply inflicted all in the name of not getting what they wanted in that very second, which they could care less about now.

Like I said, it's a roller coaster. Better yet, a roller coaster in the dark. You never know what's coming. And yet you stick with it anyway because it's fun to be scared, and the roller coaster is the time of your life. And at the end, you wouldn't change a thing.

Becoming a step-parent or adopted parent of any kind can feel like being ushered into an operating room and expected to work on a patient with heart disease when you have no medical background or training. Without having guidance in such an overwhelming situation of parenting, the ability of causing damage is inevitable if not taken seriously. If only I knew in the beginning what I know now, my children would have been able to transition better with someone understanding what they were experiencing.

Stepfathers widely find themselves in this role of mending a family and stepmothers find themselves in the role of filling a void in the father's household. This can be hard to navigate, as the need to ease the pain and give these children a real family setting is great. If you love their mother or father and are serious about the relationship, then you must see that these children are part of them. To love the parent is to love them. They need your love more than you can ever imagine. So I give this invitation to all step-parents-in-the-making to discover that this overlooked role contains magical, spiritual transformation. I invite you to become the archetype. Join me as we become the model and pattern for others to follow on our path to raising a parent as we raise our level of consciousness.

Jeremiah D. Kaynor
To Raise A Parent

Chapter 1
The Beginning of My Life

At this point it's been about three and a half years since I first met my family. 1457 days to today to be exact. I remember it like it was yesterday. But to be precise, it goes back six months before.

Out of all the people that you could pick out to be a family man, I was not the most likely candidate. Being a sponsored skateboarder, I competed a lot in my younger twenties and on October 22, I found myself at yet another competition. It was a larger one with many people there. Hectic and crowded, it was hard to find myself, to find my center. There was so much noise and music. Strangers were approaching me just to talk about the only thing that, in my mind, made people like me…skateboarding. To me, that was all people saw in me, the ability in the sport. So with that, I was very self-absorbed. I focused on the only thing I thought was important. I did not know the depth of my being, my heart, or myself.

Trying to focus on doing my best, and at the same time being pulled here and there by people I couldn't care less about, seemed to be my whole life. To be honest it made me very much alone in my head and in my world. But this time something happened that was different.

For a few seconds I became AWARE; aware of the moment, aware of the *now*. I had come across this feeling before, but only when alone in nature or away from everything and everyone. I would find myself lost in the moment when feeling the snow drop softly on my face as I looked into the gray sky, or seeing the trees as they flow so gently in the wind, and when I was watching the waves grab at the sand on a beach. But here in this mixture of organized chaos for the first time, I was truly IN THE MOMENT, I was aware of another being just as I was aware of the trees, the waves, and the snow.

I was standing next to a table, looking out over the skate park, watching the other skaters. Behind me I could hear my friend asking me something, but I was choosing to ignore him. At that moment I started to feel an emotion I was familiar with. It was the loneliness of my world that gripped me daily. I'm not sure what pulled my head to look to my right, but I did. And there she was. The most beautiful woman I had ever seen. She, at the same time, turned and looked at me. Fifty feet away and a crowd between us, we locked eyes. In that moment everything slowed to a feather falling pace. Quiet rolled over the whole place and all I saw were her eyes. It felt like I stared forever and then without warning, the energy from the smile on her face warmed my heart. She was giving. The energy from someone else, for the first time, was GIVEN to me instead of taken. She looked away and continued talking to a friend. All I could think was, *'that's the woman I want to be with'*.

Then my friend's voice, calling my name over and over, pulled me back into chaos once again.

After that day I thought a lot about the woman I had seen. I wondered if she was already in love with someone else, if she was there with a boyfriend, or maybe just a friend. Would I ever see her again? Would she ever come back to that skate park? I highly doubted it. I didn't know at the time, but I was listening to the voice in my head as it fed me negative thoughts, as I gave life to doubt. Some call this voice the ego. My ego, being so accustomed to negative emotion, (sadness, loneliness, frustration) it thrived on it, finding comfort in it.

I told a friend about her and he asked if I had approached her to talk. I think he already knew the answer, knowing that wasn't me. He just wanted to give me a hard time for not being brave. Again, this was more negative feedback. I laid awake nights and wondered who she was and how she pulled me into such an amazing moment? For months I would go back to that park and skate, hoping to see her there, not knowing what I would do or say, but just hoping for something. I realized that for the first time in my life, at that moment when I saw her, all my stress, thoughts, and negative "mind talk" had stopped. Even though it was just a moment in time, they had ceased. I wanted to understand that feeling and the moment this woman had pulled me into. I didn't get it at the time, but now I have come to know the feeling as "my center", or what my favorite term is, my Zen.

Then on May 17th 2006, she was there.

The odd thing was, on that fateful day back in October, I met her son Ryan, and (without knowing who his mother was) I had talked to him with I had NO IDEA he was going to become so dear and loved by my heart. He was almost seven at the time, a little on the quiet side, full of natural talent, and fun to talk to. He was different than all the other kids. Most kids wanted to ask if I was sponsored or how long I had been skateboarding, but he caught my attention the first time. I DO remember it well too because he stood out. I guess you could say I knew my son before I knew the rest of my family.

The same day I first saw the woman that consumed my mind, he approached me at the competition during warm ups. Instead of asking the same old questions I grew accustomed to ignoring, he asked me if I wanted to see a new trick he learned.

Right there, he grabbed my attention. It was about him. Not me. I looked down at the enthusiastic young boy and said with a smile "I would love to see a trick you learned!" And he proceeded to show me.

That day, I realized he was the son of the woman I had been wondering about. I met Dasha and we became friends. I was head over heels and she had no idea. After that day, I would ask when they would be there next, and I would do my best to be there just to see them.

I got to know Gabby, Dasha's five year old daughter in that time, too. She was yet another precious creation that stole my heart. Soon I saw that they all engulfed my thoughts daily.

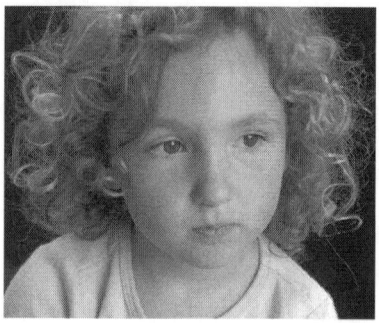

On July 4 of that year Dasha and I went on our first date. From that point on we both knew we would never be apart again. I finally found my place in life with Dasha and her two sweet children. After looking and wondering for all these years if *I would ever find the happiness that I saw others experiencing in the world*, I was

Jeremiah D. Kaynor
To Raise A Parent

there. Like a puzzle piece fitting just perfectly. But despite how much it was all worth, and how much I wanted it, little did I know how hard it would be to finish the rest of the puzzle and claim my place in the family.

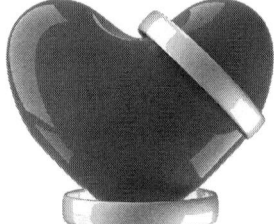

~The Beginning of Bonding~

The one important step in getting to know your children to be is bonding with them in the beginning; finding a common ground. Remember you are walking into an already set way of life with this family. This is such an important part of the journey. It's a time where you will determine the direction you are going with the mother/father and their children. How involved are you going to get? You have to understand that when you decide to step into this relationship and start the bonding period, you will have to weigh heavily the consequence of leaving it later on down the road. If you move into this relationship without understanding yourself or what the child may feel, you can make it very challenging. You have to be ready to endure the path you choose and not run at the first sign of hardship.

If you were to just leave after any sustained period with the family, you would cause more damage than you could ever imagine in the lives of the children. They will be shown it is acceptable to walk away from something if you feel it is too hard. In many cases they will see that men don't stick around as fathers, and for a young girl to pick up on this, it can be devastating to her choices in the future. You are at a significant mile marker in these children's lives if you choose to move into the bonding period.

There is a definite time where you most likely have already met the kids you are considering taking on as your own. If you have been dating their father or mother for a while, there is ample opportunity to slowly come into contact with them. That dating period is a sort of feeling out or introduction to the parent and their children. The next step you are about to take is WAY more influential in their life. Being aware of that point in the relationship, you need to be SURE that the path of parenthood is what you want to take on with this family you are about to start the joining process with. After serious contemplation, if you have not already done so, you will want to start moving into the bonding period.

The bonding period will be the beginning of the relationship with the children after you have made the decision that this is really what you want with their mother or father. This period can make every step that follows easy or hard, depending on how you enter into it. This bonding period is where you start to find your place with the child/children and slowly begin the process of taking on the responsibility of parenthood as you balance it with friendship. At first you will want to take VERY small steps into the parenting of the child. Do not overstep the fine line. Leave it almost solely to your partner for now. The balancing act in this period is difficult, but vital. Unlike a child that you've been around since day one such as a biological child, or a child that is young enough to attach him or herself to you as a parent because of dependency, this child's life is already started. This is most likely the age of four and up. You are walking into their life when they are taking on an individual outlook on life. This is the time where they are beginning to develop an ego. (I will shed light on the meaning of ego in the next chapter.)

Instead of first taking you in as a parent, they will hopefully take you in as a friend.

Someone that is fun, new, and exciting. There is a fine balance here. Even though this friendship is very important to cultivate, you need to slowly start integrating a directing, helping, teaching, PARENTING RELATIONSHIP with that friendship at the same time. This parenting relationship will be covered as we go through the book.

If you are not taken on as a friend but instead seen as a threat, you need to make sure you don't take anything personal. The best thing you can do is just be there and not pass any judgment on the situation. Let your partner work through the emotions with their child. You are not yet in the position to try and fix the emotions they are going through, but there will be a time when you will step into that role as a parent.

As you slowly start taking on the role and (as you will soon find out) "Functions" of being a parent with the qualities to direct, help, and teach, you will want to continue keeping your friendship fun with the child. Do not step into a more serious role yet. Like I said before, for now, you need to leave that up to the mother or father for now.

We all want to be the one who sweeps in and makes the kids happy, spoils them to death, buys them everything they ask for, and treat them to all sorts of fun, but doing this can hinder or even ruin the parenting relationship. Later on down the road when you need to be the parent and start to take on those parenting roles, they won't want to listen to you. It would be like one of their friends at school telling them to clean their room. You are the fun person that lets them do what they want and gives them what they want, not the one that tells them what to do or how to behave.

Remember, this isn't establishing authority. It's not instilling respect. It IS showing them you are a guiding figure in their life. You are the person who will teach them about the world and how to act in it. You are the one that can take them by the hand and help them through the darkness of the world and be their little light.

When I was first around the kids as "Mommy's boyfriend" the kids were happy. For Ryan this was unusual because since the separation and divorce of his mother and father he had been very aggressive toward men showing interest in his mom. Even at a young age. He had been a victim of a camouflaged broken home where everything seemed to be working from the exterior but was breaking down rapidly from the inside. Soon it turned into a divorce.

After the separation, his mother had to work very hard to rebuild and allow herself not to get stressed out to the maximum. It seeped out into her everyday life. She mentioned that if she had known what she knows now about meditation, spirituality, and balance, she would have known how to mend things from the inside, therefore helping shield her son from taking on so much worry and strain from the hard situation they were in.

Families that go through such a traumatic time with children at the age of understanding emotion, but not reason, create a growing mind that will reject a family institution. The synapses in a child's brain connect and cause pre-conceived concepts about reality. So they won't have the ability to see a bad situation in a family and understand it for what it is. But the pain of the emotion will still be there. When they place a misunderstood reason to the emotion, it is hard to overcome the idea programmed into their mind. Therefore, in Dasha's (my girlfriend) situation, mom plus a man equals mom being unhappy, in her son's mind.

In this situation though, there was something different. He liked the idea of his mom and me being together. After all the years of seeing her unhappy, he finally saw for the first time that she was happy. His perception of reality was that mom's unhappiness was due to her being in a relationship. This time he saw another side of reality, opening his mind to a whole new world. He was able to finally see outside the box that was created in his mind. His mother's happiness allowed him to settle, letting him come into his center. This opened up his mind, freeing it from ego long enough to dissolve his pre-conceived concept and see other possibilities outside the box. This is what I have come to call "breaking the walls of pre-conceived concepts."

Breaking down these pre-conceived concepts is a big part of growing as a step-parent and helping my family adjust to a new way of life; it has helped me understand a lot about what is real. But what is a pre-conceived concept?

Chapter 2
The Ego
The Mental "Complex"
And
The Pre-conceived Concepts

To find out how a pre-conceived concept works and gets set in place, you need to find how our wonderful minds work, and in this case, when it comes to relationships and interaction with others.

If you have ever had a chance to read any work on self-realization, spiritual or personal growth, you most likely have come to know what the ego is. As we learn how the ego works within us, that knowledge will give us a better understanding of the thinking patterns in our minds, and will shed light on the destructive thinking behavior we most often conceive as self. In this, we will also dive into what Eckhart Tolle calls the "pain body". An accumulation of pain that is a field of negative energy that occupies our mind and in many cases our bodies as well. I refer to this state of mind as a "complex" or "being in a complex".

In having understanding of both these aspects of our mind and gaining an understanding of pre-conceived beliefs, we will begin to see why and how we react to different circumstances and relationships in life. Such as being in a relationship with a partner that already has children or how we react to the steps in becoming a step-parent.

You will gain an understanding of yourself and be able to weed out the mental thicket of thorns to find the true self that lies within, the diamond in the rough, and your higher self.

Many writers and spiritual teachers speak a lot about "Pain Bodies" or complexes and the ego. One man and spiritual teacher whom I admire covers these mental aspects in his writings. His name is Eckhart Tolle. He has written some very profound books including two called The *Power of Now* and *A New Earth*. By using some of the insights in his teachings, along with teachings of others, such as Deepak Chopra, Miguel Ruiz, and more, I have been able to discover an understanding about myself.

This understanding has been my start down the path to looking within and searching for my true being or self. In turn, this has sparked another journey that parallels my own and has moved me to want to help others as they merge into an already existing family. Sometimes we will search for answers in our life and never find them while others find them and are willing to direct you to look inside yourself, so you can find the path that leads to understanding. This is the path that leads you to your higher self; to the real you. If you are truly willing to find truth and understanding, the answers to life are hidden in plain sight. All you have to do is peel back the layers that cover true understanding of life and self. Within these layers you find your true self. Spiritual teachers such as Eckhart Tolle, Deepak Chopra, Wayne Dyer, Miguel Ruiz, Diane Zimberoff, and many others are given to us to help peel back the unreal characters that hide our true self.

In finding our true self we gain the understanding it takes to give awareness to our own actions, our own feelings, and to others, such as your stepchildren. To truly be a better guide, parent, and partner, we need to find our authentic self, our true inner being, and not let it be covered by the mask of egoic personalities.

What I've learned through exploring many teachings was not who I really was, but how to FIND who I was, the real me behind the ego. I knew there was a part of me I did not understand. It was a part of my mind that didn't make sense. The reasoning behind this aspect of my mind was so off the wall with its thinking. My thoughts would make me feel at some points that *I might be quite crazy*. I didn't understand why the thoughts in my mind were so determined to be right and to make others wrong. I didn't understand how the voice, so strongly narrating negative thoughts within my head about the people I interacted with on a daily basis, could have such a powerful hold on me. I perceived what it was saying was real, then moments later, the voice would quiet down and I could see I was so far off in my reasoning. I wondered why I felt that way in the first place, as I noticed the "logic" I had been feeling and thinking earlier was ludicrous. Why had I been overlooking everything that was real just to make myself feel, either right in my frustration, or bad for myself? Why was I making myself a victim in life? What I didn't know, was the voice that always complained and felt wronged by others, was not me. Not by a long shot. It was my ego.

~True Self and the Ego~

PSYCHOLOGY Definition of Ego: *Part of mind containing consciousness:* "In Freudian psychology, one of three main divisions of the mind, containing consciousness and memory and involved with control, planning, and conforming to reality."

PHILOSOPHY Definition of Ego: *The self, especially as distinct from the world and other selves:* "The individual self, as distinct from the outside world and other selves."

What is the ego? Diane Zimberoff in her book "Longing for Belonging" had a good grasp on it when she said "As the personality develops, the *real* you – the inherent soul within – begins to associate itself with the personality and the mind. Since the function of the mind is survival, and since you begin considering that you are actually the personality, your mind begins to focus on survival of the personality. As a result, the mind tries to make the personality as strong as possible."

She brings out that, this struggle to strengthen the personality and validate it, leads to actions in life such as bragging, putting down others, striving for accomplishments that give us recognition, and later in life, striving to make a name for ourselves our legacy is not lost in death. She says, "This effort to keep the personality alive at all costs is called the ego, and this error of the mind leads to seemingly endless human suffering."

Others point to the ego as the voice in your mind, or the nonstop thinking mind. It is the voice of nonstop negativity. Like its own entity, separate from you but at the same time trying to portray itself as you, and in almost every case, you will believe its deception until you are aware of it. But if you stop to observe the voice as it complains about a situation in life or another person, you will start to get a glimpse of your true self.

Spiritual teachers in the world and people that have come to understand this aspect of the human mind, point out that you, or the "higher self" is the one listening to that voice. You are listening to the ego as it flows, nonstop like a river. Eckhart Tolle asks the question, "When you have the incessant negative voice complaining in your mind, who is listening?" He answers, "You are."

But how can there be two of us inside our head? Are we all insane? Well, maybe to a point we are. If we listen to this ego that seems to always have something negative to remark or complain about, we may as well be insane.

I once worked with a man who always walked around talking to himself out loud in his native tongue. Everyone around him was scared of him and thought he was quite crazy. One day I finally asked him who he was talking to and what he was saying. He looked at me with amusement, as if it was such an obvious answer and said, "I talk to myself. I talk about how little time I have to get my work done and how much work there is to do. It passes the day away quicker."

I smirked and asked if he ever answered himself, and he looked at me with casual eyes and shrugged, "Sometimes. Mostly I just listen."

When others inquired about what he had told me and if he was crazy, I replied, "No, he just thinks out loud."

I did not know the significance of his answer at the time, but later I came to understand the deeper meaning of its truth. We all think and talk to ourselves, if not out loud, in our own heads. And if someone says, "No I don't! There is no voice in my head!" Right there is the voice. The ego is giving its answer.

How do you turn it off? You don't. You just become aware of it.

In the "Power of Now" I came to understand how to become aware of the egoic voice that I perceived as me. As many times as I have gone over the understandings that Eckhart Tolle has laid out for people to read, I am still learning. Every day I grow closer to understanding, to awareness, to myself. It is a struggle at times but I still strive for it. In turn, I have grown closer to my family, closer to my lover, closer to my stepchildren.

My stepdaughter once replied when asked if she could notice the difference from the voice that complained in her head from the one that was listening, "Yes, but the one that listens has a voice, too. It's much quieter, almost hard to hear."

At the age of seven she already had the ability to understand this. Matter of fact, she took it a stepfarther and mentioned the true self had a voice, but it was hard to hear over the egoic voice. She was right though. The voice of the true self is there. Quiet as it may be, it is the voice that many call the "Voice of the Higher Self".

Learning to quiet ego is what many strive for. By being aware of the ego you take away the power it has, leaving it to slowly dissolve. As it dissolves, the voice of the higher self becomes more noticeable.

Here is an example of a situation you might find familiar. With it, you can gain a little insight into how a common ego can react to normal adolescent behavior:

A father is trying to get a child to do their homework. The child, being young and needing guidance, does everything to avoid the homework like many children do. After asking many times the father starts to get irritated with the situation. In his head he is most likely hearing a commentary of *"Why is he/she so lazy? Why can't they respect me when I ask them to do something? Is it SO hard for* them to just once do what I ask the first time? I swear to God, if I have to say it again."

Soon enough the father speaks the negative commentary out loud with a forceful voice, yelling at the child, shouting threats of grounding or no dinner. The child jumps to attention, starts crying or complaining, which then sets off their little ego as it either fights back with the fathers ego, or in most cases it ends up just shattering, thus creating a new complex.

Later on he may calm down and the ego will subside, or he may look back to see other ways he could have handled it better. This is the voice of the higher self. If he were to give awareness to the ego as it first arose, he could have avoided the whole problem. The voice of the higher self may have said, "I wonder if they need help with their homework. They are avoiding it for other reasons. What's their mood? Do they need to burn off some energy from sitting at school all day? Are they moping around like something might be weighing heavily on their minds? Could something have happened at school to make them feel bad and not want to focus?"

By listening to the voice of the higher self and being centered in your true self, it opens up your vision to see the realities in life around you. Instead of letting the ego run negative thoughts through your head, it allows you to be open and understanding.

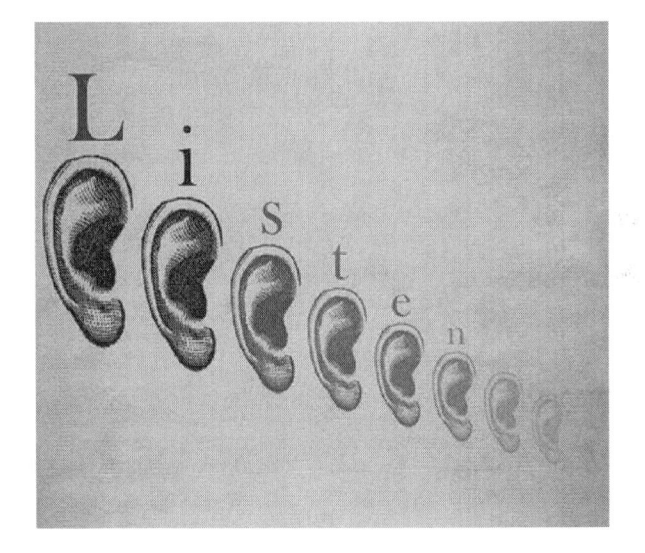

Jeremiah D. Kaynor
To Raise A Parent

~The Complex~

A Definition of "Complex": A system of interrelated, emotionally charged ideas, feelings, memories, and impulses that are usually repressed gives rise to abnormal or pathological behavior so complicated or intricate as to be hard to understand or deal with.

In PSYCHOLOGY: *"A complex is a group of unconscious associations connected by a recognizable theme, or a strong unconscious impulse lying behind an individual's otherwise mysteriously negative condition."*

This mental state has been referred to in many ways, but the name I have come to use for this mental moment, or thinking behavior is "Complex".

Sigmund Freud first talked about the complex when it came to psychology, then his close associate, Carl Jung, took the understanding of a complex to another level. The human mind, when in a complex, has so much emotion and memory wrapped up in it. It is too complicated to be logical and does not make sense to anyone who may be observing from the outside. Because within a complex is complication.

Eckhart Tolle speaks of a state of mind and body that is similar to the complex. He calls it the Pain Body.

One description of the Pain Body I found is "Reflections On Eckhart Tolle's Concept Of The Pain Body" by Saleem Rana. Referring to the Pain Body, he says: "As ego arising from thoughts of limitations, fracturing itself against obstacles it encounters, it develops what Eckhart Tolle calls the "Pain Body". The Pain Body then becomes an **unconscious** entity within. It seeks to feed on pain to survive. It makes a person feel pain and it causes this person to inflict pain on others."

Eckhart Tolle, in *The Power of Now* says, "There are two levels of pain: the pain that you create now, and the pain of the past that still lives on in your mind and body. This of course includes the pain that you suffered as a child, caused by the unconsciousness of the world into which you were born. The accumulated pain is a negative energy field that occupies your body and mind. If you look at it as an invisible entity in its own right, you are getting quite close to the truth. It's the emotional Pain Body."

I have come to understand that when this Pain Body comes up, you are in a state of complex, putting you in a state full of complication.

My wife told me she understood how complicated one's thinking could be when in complex. She became aware of a complex and observed it as the emotions came up within her. It happened when she learned that her mother was babysitting her sister's puppy. She said a flood of emotions came up and she was instantly thinking back to past issues with her own mother. The memories and emotions she had were not at all associated with her mother watching her sister's puppy, but somewhere within that conversation, her ego latched onto a feeling and brought up a complex that made her feel upset. Her ego felt wronged and thought, "She never was there for me when I was working full time and needed my kids to be watched while I went through the divorce."

She knew that anyone else would have thought watching the puppy was a nice gesture on her mother's part, but for reasons that were *complicated* and had no association to the present conversation, she felt upset. It was irrational thinking, but he was in complex. The reasons for that complex lived only in the past where her perception was that she had no support during her divorce. The feelings had nothing to do with the present, so she had one advantage in the moment; she was aware she was in complex. This gave her the chance to look deeper into the source of the complex and work on releasing it all together.

Like the definition of complex stated: "A system of interrelated, emotionally charged ideas, feelings, memories, and impulses that are usually repressed gives rise to abnormal or pathological behavior."

Her negative emotions or feelings were coming up due to memories or old repressed feelings, not because of her knowledge of events. The conversation was just an excuse that the ego used to bring up the feelings and emotions.

An example of how a complex could be born would be this: A child is pushed around at school by an older child making the younger person feel small and helpless. This is a seed that starts the growth of a complex. In turn, the child returns home and sooner or later proceeds to torment the younger sibling, or does things to show he is bigger and more superior to his smaller sibling. This makes the child feel better and feeds the complex, so that the pain of feeling small and helpless seems to diminish, for the time being. Soon the child starts to disobey and goes against everything he is told to do. In their mind, they're not letting anyone control them or push them around. As the child grows into an adult, he becomes the one that pushes people around when he feels threatened or perceives he is being threatened in any way. This makes him feel superior to others. He becomes strong willed and stubborn as he goes against the grain of all others around him in life. He may even start to perceive this stubborn person as his identity in life. One day he is confronted with his partner telling him she will no longer accept some of his behavior. He needs to change it, or it will no longer work out between them. He gets upset and feels she is wrong. His thinking may go along the lines of, "Who is she to be telling me that I need to change? She is the one who needs to work on herself. She thinks she can tell me what to do and how to be? I can do or act however I want." He is in complex.

The complex will continue to come up and overtake the person until the complex is given awareness. He would need to become aware of it and look deeper into why he gets upset over someone telling him what to do or how to be. The truth is, when a person finds offense in something people say or do, it usually has nothing to do with that moment, but more with past experiences.

When you find yourself feeling heavy negative emotions you just can't get past, your mind won't move on from them, and they seem like a skipping record, this is your mind residing in a complex.

I found that a complex tends to act out heavily in relationships where a non-biological child resides. Why wouldn't they? In a perfect ecosystem as this kind of relationship, they are given ample feeding opportunities. The most common complex, found in this type of relationship, grows from the pre-conceived notions that the child you are growing a bond with, will never love you as a real parent. The complex can make you feel like they couldn't ever really love you because they are not yours.

At times, you may hear a child lash out with, "You are not my father! You can't tell me what to do!" This, in itself, is a complex, or "pain body" within the child, trying to feed as the ego looks to gain control in their world. This will easily spark your own complex, leading to both complexes feeding off each other's negative reactions.

Ultimately this is the only thing the ego wants in a relationship; control. If the ego perceives it is losing control, then it will fight back. A complex will waken and try to balance out the field by causing emotional pain to the one it perceives took its control. The two complexes will continue to collide with each other until one or the other is exhausted and the body it resides in can't take it anymore. As the weaker ego backs down from exhaustion and the complex falls back into dormancy, the body will feel drained of energy. This will not stop. It will occur over and over until one person will recognize the mental state they are in is a complex. As they do, their awareness will start to take away its power. This is a good time for the person to look at the feelings they are having, understand they are not real but they are more or less defensive for complicated reason. It is a complex you are in and it is not your true self. If, in the moment, you think, "It IS me! I do feel that way. I feel hurt, betrayed, pushed around, and not listened to. I have the right to be upset." Then this is the complex and ego talking and you have not yet stepped out of that state of ego. Until you can recognize this is NOT the true self, you will continue to suffer in these relationships.

When you start to be involved as a step-parent in the relationship, complexes will manifest with ease in your life. The feeling of being betrayed by the partner you love, due to their past and the fact they were with somebody else, or the feeling of not being taken serious as a parental figure tends to be perfect feeding grounds for complexes. In this relationship you must be aware of your egoic thinking and complexes, or they will overwhelm and tear apart your relationship before it gets a good solid foundation.

Complexes make us suffer strong emotional distress and if not given awareness, could surely cause one to act out toward another or the relationship itself. The complex makes us feel hurt or wounded, and in return, we will try to lash out against the ones we feel have wronged us, including others that may be in our path. This can be devastating to a child in the wake of a complex you might be in, and you can be sure it will create a complex in that child. Many children get their complexes from their parents. Can you imagine a stepfather (or stepmother) who is unaware of his complex as it comes up to cause its own pain and pain to others? Emotionally striking back with words and actions seems to be the most popular way to feed the complex as it makes others feel the same as, if not worse, than it does you. Just as the child's complex comes up if he or she has something taken away from him or her, so does a grown adults when they feel wronged by a lack of attention, feelings of not being listened to, or feelings of being betrayed (widely founded by assumption and misinterpretation of the mind in most cases).

CAUTION

EASILY OFFENDED

~ Pre-conceived Concepts~

A Definition of a Concept: Something thought or imagined; *"Something that somebody has thought up or that somebody might be able to imagine."*

2nd Definition of a Concept: Broad principle affecting perception and behavior; *"A broad abstract idea or a guiding general principle, e.g. one that determines how a person or culture behaves or how nature, reality, or events are perceived."*

A pre-conceived concept is an aspect of thinking that limits us from seeing life for what it really can be, and what really is. I have thought a lot about how we all grow up with these ideas that are planted in our head and seem to completely obstruct our sight so we cannot see outside the box.

It started when my father, being quite the mathematician, showed me a mathematical problem that later I passed on to my high school math teacher. My teacher said at first glance it didn't seem possible, but my father was right. He figured out a better way of solving the problem by thinking outside the box. The math teacher said that conventional teaching of math would never cover such a way of thinking. It was too deep or "too far outside the box" for people. This made me wonder, how many other things we were taught that could potentially limit us from being able to think in less conventional ways?

As I grew older the idea soon fled my mind and I forgot what I learned. But one day I was driving my two stepchildren to school when I heard an eccentric DJ on the radio say, and I quote, "No man could EVER love a stepchild the way he would love his OWN biological child. In fact he could never have any affection for a child that was not his."

This about tore my heart out, I was so hurt that the world would tell me that the children I was so in love with, the kids I held as close to my heart as my own, the very children listening in the back seat of the car could never really be loved by me. How could someone think such a thing? Was the love I felt so strongly not worth recognizing because I was just a step-parent? How could people think this? It was such a slap in my face by society and even though my stepson spoke out and said "I doubt that man has children or even stepchildren of his own, or he wouldn't say that" the words still struck a deep pain within me.

Later on I was looking through one of the children's books with my stepdaughter, and it had the story of Cinderella in it. Looking at the pictures I saw an image that jolted my mind into realization. The "Wicked Stepmother" concept hit me.

Here we live in a world and society that imprints the idea of step-parents being wicked, unloving, and mean to their non-biological children. We teach that same concept to our children through bedtime stories and movies.

When I was younger, kids would jokingly repeat the horrific saying "Beaten like a red headed stepchild" when speaking of getting beat in a confrontation. Even movies showing step-parents trying to ship off their stepchildren soon after the marriage, portrays a negative outlook.

Do you remember the story of "Hansel and Gretel" and how the stepmother was cruel to the children? Her "bewitching powers" seemed to render the loving father helpless. The wicked stepmother was placed in the story as a very bad person that seemingly took control of the family and sent the children out into the forest alone to their demise. This was something the father would never have permitted if it were not for his new wife taking over.

Do I have to even mention the Cinderella or Snow White stories?

No wonder people such as the DJ on the radio would think there was no way a step-parent could love a stepchild. The DJ himself most likely felt it could be no other way. We teach our children from an early age that it's something to be feared. When we are living in a society with a 50% divorce rate, what do we expect from the families who try to build off of a broken home? It was predicted by 2010 there would be more stepfamilies than nuclear families in the U.S., so what chance do we give our future when led by these teachings?

The step-parents are entering a situation with the preconceived concept that he or she will be viewed as a "wicked step-parent" and will therefore unconsciously fall into that role. This is what I have called "wicked step-parent" syndrome.

But what if it was possible to recognize and become aware of these thought patterns. Could you overcome them? How does one come to understand and see the existence of a "thought" or concept as not being real when you already have it imprinted in your mind and thinking pattern? I still did not have a grasp on how a preconceived concept worked and how much they controlled ones view of life. This came to me later in the oddest way.

I wanted to brush my teeth and while standing next to Dasha at the sink, I was looking for my toothbrush. I scanned and scanned the counter for it to no avail. I saw Dasha's toothbrush standing there upright like they were designed to do, but mine was nowhere to be found. "Have you seen my toothbrush, Ami?" I asked.

"No. Where did you put it last?" she answered me.

I got frustrated with myself for not remembering where I had put it. Then Dasha stopped what she was doing for a moment and looked down to point it out. It was laying right next to the toothpaste in plain sight. "How in the WORLD could I have missed that?" I thought to myself.

I had looked all over the counter. It was impossible for me to miss something that was in plain sight. Then it hit me. I had looked at Dasha's toothbrush standing up. This in turn imprinted in my head that mine HAD to be standing upright just as hers, so I was looking for it standing up.

The more frustrated I got, the harder it was for me to open up to see outside the box. It was imprinted so quickly it made me blind to the possibility of it laying down and by letting my irritation take a hold of me it clouded my perception even farther. I COULD NOT see outside the box at ALL. And what was outside the box my egoic frustration was holding me to? Outside the box are possibilities.

But if possibilities are outside the box, then what is inside? Could the only thing in the box that limits us to narrow thinking be our own ego? Could this be why it makes us see the world through assumptions and judgment? I, for one, feel this is the case.

The ego, being so closed off to open ideas, uses the first thing it is introduced to and takes it as reality. That is why, when in an argument, your ego can't see what is really going on. It is holding onto anything it can to prove what it perceives as right. It is only later when the ego calms down and the authentic self-steps in that you can see what is really going on.

The only thing that can really see outside the box is the true self. This tells you how much we live in the egoic state of thinking. I started to see how our minds or ego are so susceptible to these pre-conceived concepts that they could take control within seconds, clouding our minds from reality.

Jeremiah D. Kaynor
To Raise A Parent

~My Troubling Ego~

I ran into this problem with MY ego. The ego would take pre-conceived concepts and hold onto them, holding me back from being the parent that was needed with my stepson. In letting my ego control my emotions and cloud reality from my mind, I caused a lot of frictional web-weaving between me and my stepson that had to later be undone. If I had just taken the time to be aware of my ego and see what was really happening, I could have side-stepped a lot of hard work in our relationship. We would have been stronger as a father and son from the beginning.

I want you to pay attention to this next example of ego on my part. It shows how a strong ego, coupled with a complex, can cloud reality in times of parenting. You will see how my ego reacted to the normal ego of a child and his complex. In fact you will see how my complex fed off the complex of my stepson. You may find yourself in these moments or in moments that seem very similar, but remember, if you are aware of your ego, it can't act out in the way you are about to see in this next example. By giving full presence and awareness to your child you can shrink his or her ego as well and have clearer, more constructive communication with them.

As you read through this I will also be giving you insight into what to expect from your stepchild's ego and mental complexes as well as explain how a child's ego can and will react to situations. It will give explanations of why the egos react in this manner and all this will help you to be the understanding step-parent they need in their life. So again, pay attention. It's one of the understandings I wish I had known from the start:

Ryan, being a normal kid, would get upset and act out when it came to anything he didn't want to do. By going through such a hard period in his early years with the divorce and all he witnessed from his parents, he had a lot of pent up frustration and anger. At his age, he didn't know how to deal with it and this would amplify his resistance to parenting.

You will most likely find that children who go through harder divorces and break ups will have emotions, complexes, and misconceptions they don't quite know how to deal with. This is where being a good parent who is understanding and aware comes into play, and is needed on even a greater scale. They need you to guide them through and to be present with them as their complexes come up to feed off their emotions. You, as a step-parent can help them if you are aware. If not, you could hinder their emotional growth and set them up for a hard road ahead. I know you want to be aware and to be the step-parent they need because you are here, reading this book.

All kids try to resist what they don't want by pushing back in an effort to get their own way. To test where your boundaries are is a natural process in growing up. Children will constantly test the waters here and there to see what they can get, or get away with. That is why, as parents, you need to be consistent with them and teach them that getting upset about things won't get them what they want in life. I for one fell short of this and let my ego take personal offense to Ryan's actions as a child.

You can't get upset or angry at children for trying to get what they want. We, as adults, let our egos do the same thing, but in a more unobserved way. For example, most of us in the beginning of our relationships, will feel out situations to see what we can and can't get away with. It seems to be a common action for an ego to act out this way, as if it were a child looking for its boundaries. So how can we get upset with our children for doing essentially the same thing? It's not their true self acting that way but the little egos within them saying "I am being wronged by being forced to do this, so if I act out, maybe I will prove myself right and in control of my world."

It is kind of amusing when you become aware of it and just observe the egos actions of desperation trying to get its own way. It is also a great mirror for yourself to understand a little about how your own ego works. When this happens, it is important to BE AWARE and not let your ego react like you will see how mine reacted. We need to have understanding with them instead of feeding their ego with energy from ours.

I found that being aware and having understanding is harder than you would imagine when you have an ego as strong as mine was. At times, my ego at times was so strongly offended by having a child not listen to me, I would have a problem seeing the real issue was outside the box. Sometimes this would last for days. This would stop me from grasping the reality of a situation and would NOT allow me to be understanding of my stepson's actions. It would kick in the instant my stepson would sigh, roll his eyes, throw his hands up, be irritable, or get upset and start to whine over being asked to do something. His ego was acting out to see if it could get away with pushing things to the point where it didn't have to do what it was told. This is completely normal reaction for a child's ego. That's where consistent parenting is needed to guide them.

This is where I was struggling for so long. My ego would hold onto the pre-conceived concept of, "This child won't listen to me because I am not his REAL dad and therefore he has NO respect for me as a parent and never will."

This is where I needed to be aware of my own ego and complexes thus being consistent with him and teaching him. But I wasn't for quite a while.

What was amazing was not how strong my ego was in the mode of feeling offended by any little situation, but rather, this pre-conceived concept which came from something I was taught, along with an old complex that had lived within me. This complex was telling me over and over that I was not good enough to be listened to. It was a complex of feeling unworthy I had struggle with for years. I was shocked to find the ego could help give birth to its own pre-conceived concept about life just to feed a complex. But that's just what my mind had done.

My ego made me think that because he was not my "REAL" child, he was not going to do what I asked and would throw a fit if I even attempted to say anything. My ego would feel offended and say "Never mind, I will just do it myself. I don't even know why I asked." And it would say this without ever giving him a chance. To make it worse, at times when he would be in a low or irritable mood and get upset over any little thing, my ego would react and take on blame just so it could feed the complex, thus taking on the victim role. My ego would speak out and say things like, "I know you hate me because I'm not your real father." This was very damaging to a parent child relationship all because I was not aware of two egos feeding off of each other. Mine feeding a complex and his feeding the ego to make it feel in control. Plus I was not being understanding or aware with him at all.

I was letting my ego blind me to the real problems. Later, for instance, I started realizing most of the times he came home from school in an irritable mood, it was due to the fact something had happened at school to bother him. If I had been aware of my ego and the complexes it fed, I would have been more open to understanding what he might be going through, therefore, asking him if something was weighing heavy on his mind. Instead, I jumped to the conclusion it was my fault he was upset, or he was just annoyed with my being around. It would have also made it easier on him to build that part of the relationship where he felt open and safe to talk to me about things that bothered him. Unfortunately at that time I was not being the stepfather I needed to be.

I was completely blinded by what my ego had put in my head and it got stuck in that narrow minded box for quite awhile. Every time he pushed a little to test the boundaries, or was in a low mood, my ego would pop up the sign with its pre-conceived concept written all over it. The made me feel unheard, unworthy, un-respected, and fed the complex within.

Our actions and reactions did NOTHING to shrink our egos, but one day while sitting alone, meditating on what was happening and trying to figure out why it was happening, I hit upon a realization. I realized my ego was feeding the complex. In order to feed it, it had to make up a reason for me to react to Ryan's ego, so it planted a pre-conceived concept to keep my mind within the confines of the egoic box. In this case, it had MORE than enough food to feed its complex.

When I became aware of this, it shined a light on the way I was looking at my relationship with my stepson. I became aware of his ego and how it was working. I could almost see when it would come and go. It was like watching a light go on and off. With that I was aware of MY ego, how it was reacting, and why. It was hard to give it presence at first because it was such a loud egoic reaction within my mind, but at least I was able to see it for what it was. With that, my reactions to his ego started to change. I would become aware of my ego and what it was doing more quickly as it came up. This allowed me to quiet my ego faster and start to work through my complexes, thus becoming more of an understanding parent than a reactive egoic parent. If I could work through my complexes, it would help me be more of a consistent parent, who could teach him instead of hindering his growth as a human in this world.

When you can look at life openly and clear your mind of ego, you will be able to see these pre-conceived concepts for what they are. Whether they are taught to us or planted by our own ego in order to feed complex, they are unreal notions in our thought patterns.

My family met a man named Greg Dambour who gave spiritual tours of the vortexes in Sedona, Arizona. He told me that when you're in a low mood, feeling bad, or offensive about a situation, stop and ask yourself "How can I look at this differently?"

This is a beautiful, easy way of opening up your mind to reality. It's simple and yet makes you observe a situation so you can work through the pre-conceived concept until you see it for what it really is. When meditating on your previous reactions to a problem situation, ask yourself the same thing.

"How could I have looked at that in a different way?" And when you find your answer, look to see what stopped you from seeing it the first time. You will most likely find where your pre-conceived concepts lay and will be able to open your mind from them, freeing yourself and the relationship with your stepchild.

~Common Complexes and Egoic Actions~

To tell you the truth, when I started dating Dasha, things went really good for a while. The kids and I got along great. I spoiled them and they loved having me around. Ryan said that he liked the fact his mom was happy. It helped that Ryan and I had a common bond; Skateboarding. Later on, this became a division between us because I was unaware, as you will find out. But all in all, days were good and I was happy, so I thought. Well, to say it right, I was happy, but things were stirring inside and feelings I didn't understand or know how to work through, were starting to sprout up.

There are a few major emotions or complexes that will come up in every new relationship. The complex along with the ego will thrive in trying to build itself up in ways if not noticed, will crush the relationship and all who are involved. The only way to ensure they will not have an effect on YOU and the relationship is by being aware of them. Having understanding of them will give you insight on how to keep them from running rampant in the relationship with your new family.

I had many of these emotions and complexes come up in the beginning when my ego would try to build itself up to compensate for its low view of self. Fabricating, stretching and avoiding truth were ways my ego would try to fit in and make itself feel more similar to those around me.

Jealousy of people from the past, feelings of "not good enough", wanting to be the center of attention, wanting to feel like a leader, wanting to feel like the only one, and trying to find identity in the person you are with (finding yourself in this person), all these emotions and wants can be fairly strong without you knowing it. Add children into the mix and the emotions are a flood that sweeps you away. They are ALL ego based thoughts and complexes will feed them if not put in check to be looked at for what they are. NOT REAL. If you do not take the time to understand them, to see them for what they really are, and to find their source, you will not be a successful a partner or parent.

You will want to be able to face each complex and egoic eruption in seclusion, one at a time. That will not happen. You will feel one complex attack one day and all the others the next day, or they will fall on you like dominoes. One won't come up for weeks and then as soon as you feel like you made it through, it will be back stronger than ever with two more to egg it on. Any little word or action can pull you into them. This is the struggle that the ego has with love. Anything that comes out of ego is not love. How can it be? With that intense "love", comes intensely hurt feelings, intense confusion, and intense frustration. This is not where true love derives. Love comes from outside these emotions. It transcends the ego and complexes, giving a moment of pure truth. That is real love toward another.

Chapter 3
Faces of the Ego: Jealousy, Control, and Identity

Diane Zimberoff brings out in her book "Longing for Belonging" that the ego seeks to stay alive through six different angles. "(1) competing; (2) validating its own point of view and invalidating other peoples point of view; (3) making itself right and others wrong; (4) justifying its own behavior; (5) judging the behavior of others; (6) self-aggrandizing."

As you can see, in a family atmosphere where you are a step-parent there are plenty of opportunities for the ego to strive and keep the "personality strong." Competition breeds jealousy and envy.

Jeremiah D. Kaynor
To Raise A Parent

~The Face of Jealousy~

Jealousy is a condition of the mind that everyone is capable of, and as far as I know, everyone suffers from it, if not in a subtle way, in a more prevalent one. Starting out when we are children, while we gain identities with objects and people in life, we learn this condition early on when we feel that OUR parents or OUR friends should be ours and ours alone. Due to this we may feel pains of jealousy come up when they pay attention to another child or another friend. If someone has something that the perceived "I" wants, or plays with a toy that is viewed as "MINE", we can again feel that pain of the condition called jealousy.

Why is this? What makes us feel so hurt when an object is taken, shared unwillingly, or not possessed by you? Or when a loved one shows love to another, instead of feeling happy that another human is receiving affection, why do we feel unhappy that it is not us? Eckhart Tolle points out that we find identity in things. MY car, MY house, MY toy, MY family and so on. We feel these things make up who we are. Therefore who we think we are, is threatened when these things are taken or given to someone else. This condition plays a KEY factor in making it hard to be a step-parent AND in being a partner. Being aware of this will save you much heartache.

First, let us look at the most common areas that the jealousy condition will arise in the family, not only for you, but for your stepchild, too. When I first started getting to know the kids as part of my life, their father was not as much a part of their lives. He was there, but at that time he was just starting to try and show he had taken the steps in life to fix his problems, and be part of his kids' lives. Truthfully, I could not want anything more than to have the children be able to have their biological father in their life, so they would be able to be proud of him, know he loved them, and not feel abandoned. I could not imagine having a father who didn't want to be a big part of my life. So, for that reason, I really wanted to see him step up into their life.

But, at the same time, I had these strong feelings that would overwhelm me like a storm coming in and taking over the sky. They would flood into my life as if they had real reason to be concerned about the situation. Feelings of being unloved or not loved as much, feelings of having something taken away, feelings of not ever being good enough, and feelings of pain would arise for reasons that seemed SO real. Reasons that seemed SO unfixable, SO hard to overcome, SO concretely secured in life, it was almost like I was stupid for even thinking I could face them. They made me feel like I should give up, like it was pointless to try. All of these feelings that came up so powerfully were linked to two things; two ideas that are real in their own way, but in reality, are alive only in the mind.

One was a pre-conceived concept I had placed in my head. The concept was this: *The kids will never accept me as a father figure because they resent me for being with their mother instead of their real dad being with her.*

The other problem was an ego based complex that was born years before in my childhood. This complex filled my head with ideas of not being good enough, not being capable of succeeding, and feelings of not deserving. A conception and "complex" so unreal, but in my mind it was very real. They held power over me by tricking my thinking into believing they were truth and fact. The complex and pre-conceived concept clouded my perception of life. I would only see what they wanted me to see, so they could continue to feed and grow stronger off of the negative energy my mind would create.

Jeremiah D. Kaynor
To Raise A Parent

~The Face of Identity~

A Definition of Identity: Essential self; *"The set of characteristics that somebody recognizes as belonging uniquely to himself or herself and constituting his or her individual personality for life."*

Have you ever been angry at another person for using YOUR property without asking? Have you been upset when you lost something you felt was of great value even when it was worth nothing to others? What if someone takes something that belongs to you, how do you react? Do you feel wronged by the situation?

These are just some of the everyday situations you can look to and see how your ego finds identity in things. Ego tends to create identity in owning, or belonging. In all truth, if looked at, the things your ego searches out identity in can never come close to being "who" you are, or even explaining the person/personality you are inside. People hold on to physical things, material things, and accomplishments as if these things are what adds meaning to their life, and tells or shows others what kind of person they are inside. Here is a strong example of this.

I was in a car with a friend of mine coming back from a dinner at his parents. While we were driving on the freeway, a man and his wife in their early fifties were racing through traffic in a brand new $120,000 Porsche. As he tried to pass my friend and cut into the traffic at 90 MPH, he came within inches of hitting the center median. Over correcting the sports car, he spun around and slid back across the four lanes of traffic, slamming into the wall and flipping over. The car had its top down and slid upside down for some ways until coming to a stop in the center of the freeway. We got out and ran to help. As I pulled the man from under the car, another motorist helped his wife on the other side. She was frantic and bleeding from the head.

You would think the man would rush to his wife's side to be there for her in such a terrifying moment, but instead he paced back and forth yelling over and over "MY life is OVER! I wrecked my baby! How could I have done this?" This was the ego being diminished by having its identity taken from it.

The man was so wrapped up in his identity with the sports car he didn't even care about his wife or her well-being. He sincerely felt his life was less because he lost such a material vehicle. To him it was as if his life was being threatened, coming to an end, now that he was without this car. He found his identity in this expensive "THING". This was the first time I had ever witnessed such an ordeal in another person, or at least became aware of it. Granted, it was on a large scale that this man was consumed by identity with the car, so it was a little easier to see the ego react in such a way, but it wasn't until later that I came to understand it.

We all find identity in things. Feeling we are less if they are lost or taken from us. But can ANYTHING in this world be credited for having the ability to describe the BEING you are? Could ownership of something or belonging to something ever portray the awesome way your body breaths on its own, the miracle of how your cells work together to sustain life without your mindful direction, or the capability of feeling love and appreciation for creation?

If you sit down and meditate on the greatness that you are and the amazement that is YOU as a creation, in the end, could you find a possession that mirrored you perfectly in life? What could ever compare to the depth of your complexity? Could owning something paint an accurate depiction of your being? What about knowing of and the interaction with another person? Could this tell how amazing your existence is, or does it just build up the ego within them and within you?

What if you belonged to a society or group? Does this describe you as an individual creation, blooming daily with every breath in all its glory? Does belonging to a family build up your true self or just the ego? If you take time to quiet the voice that is the ego and answer from your higher self, you will find all of the questions of course, sound absurd. Nothing and NO FORM (as some refer to the physical world outside of the mind and spirit) could ever REALLY describe you. You just are. You are above all that is form. You are creation at its most beautiful.

So why do we still strive to find identity in a world of form? You can even find identity in being a parent to your stepchildren and in some cases, being with your partner. If you look at yourself and feel that now you are a stepfather, a stepmother, and this is what defines you, you are still taking identity in the family and that being a step-parent is who you are in life. If you feel diminished inside when hearing someone talk lesser of a step-parent than of a bio-parent, then you are finding identity in the children and in being a step-parent. The truth is, you are no less than anyone on this earth, just as no one is less than you. The only thing that judges itself against others is ego. Ego is the ONLY THING that sees the world as something it has to conquer or become greater than everything in it. So it is ego finding its identity in the new family you have and it is very hard to separate the ego from things when it comes to being a step-parent.

When we enter a new family and start a life with them, we tend to attach to them in ways that can only be described as "ego pleasing". To be attached in a loving manner is not wrong in its own right, but there are ways we can attach (when seen from a clear and aware mind) when derived from ego and not love.

We can feel like our identity as a parent is threatened by another, or at least our ego is feeling it is being threatened. The ego will almost always perceive a threat when it comes to the biological parent at first. I know any of you just starting into this relationship knows what I am talking about. The jealousy and feelings of having what you are now a part of (this family or relationship) threatened are in the beginning of ALL relationships. If you move into a relationship with somebody and their past partner, or even a friend of the opposite sex, is there in the picture, you get the SAME feelings of jealousy and worry to some point. Then, as you become secure in the relationship and boundaries are established, you realize you don't feel that nervous "what if they leave me" feeling as much. In some cases, it seems to go away all together. That's because you KNOW your partner loves you and the understanding of their love tears down doubt.

This can be true with your stepchildren as well. In the beginning, you may feel when attention is given to the biological parent, you are less of a father/mother or person to the children. This can come up even if the children talk about their other parent. It's because the feelings of wanting to be their only real father or mother are strong. Why is it strong? It is because the ego trying to grab for identity in being a parent and in being loved by the children. Coupled with jealousy, this can be a hard thing to let go of.

You love them and want them to give you love back. This is normal. The only problem is, if you find identity in being a parent you will want them to love ONLY you as the father or mother and your ego will feel bad when they don't. If you look at who you are, you will see these new people in your life don't define you. Father/mother is just a function you are fulfilling at the time to give guidance and direction. Functions are necessary roles that are played out in life. You are not defined by these functions. Eckhart Tolle brings out the answer to "Who am I?" is just that. It is not "I am the parent of so and so, a building designer, and a great chef on the barbecue." Those are just functions the ego gets identity from. The answer is in the question. "I AM".

Once I understood this answer I started to get a better grasp on understanding myself. It took me awhile to fully comprehend that there was nothing in this world worth downgrading my identity. The fact I just existed was far more amazing than anything I could do, say, or be in life.

So by understanding the way the ego acts out and how it views the world of form in the beginning of the relationship, you will be able to move into the relationship with open eyes and an open heart. This will lead to being able to give guidance much easier and in a loving manner when it comes to the children you are taking on as your own.

The other place people tend to find or lose identity is with their partner. Some will try to become the same as their lover. Not ALL couples do this, but it seems to occur often. It often happens in smaller ways that go unnoticed by observers. This is not a completely bad thing, but if you start to lose yourself in the other person, then it becomes a problem. This usually happens to the weaker ego. It will try to adapt to the stronger ego in the relationship and eventually both will recognize the lack of authenticity as the two egos clash, fighting for survival and dominance.

At some point, you may look at your life and say, "This is not me. I don't even know who I am anymore." You don't ever want this to happen because this is when you or your partner will feel you are not the one they married.

You need to be true to yourself, by being authentic to whom you are. Don't try to adopt your partner's identity and life. They are attracted to you in life for a reason. You might share a lot in common, but don't let go of the things that make you unique. For the most part you will find that is why they are with you. The things they feel set you apart are the things they most likely love about you.

~Function VS. Identity~

Through meditation and searching I have learned if you look at yourself for who you really are, you will find your identity is nothing close to what you do in life. What you DO just seems to be a function of the moment and even that seems to change moment to moment depending on what is needed from you. If you were a parent or even a father or mother 100% of the time you would not find the time to be the friend you also need to be. These are all functions or roles you play out when the moment is in need of them.

Sometimes the moment may call for you to let go of the function and role of being a parent and let the child have a little slack to be their own person. You will notice these moments come more often as your children get older. You will need to (at points) slowly let go of the parental function of the child as they grow into a young adult. Then you will see the friend function move into the more prominent role. As your children grow up, being there for them on their level as a friend can be more effective at times than trying to be a parent reprimanding them in times of wrongful choice making. You do not need to always be the parent just because that's the title you hold.

It is also important to know that the love and success of your children does not prove how good a parent you are to them. That is proven by your actions. If you know you ARE a good parent and feel truly happy about how you are raising the children, that's the first indicator you are on the right path with them. After sincere contemplation, if you feel you are not doing your best at being a father or mother due to falling short of responsibility, then you will know there is a change you need to make. When I say "sincere contemplation", I mean you need to observe your life without being in an egoic state. I suggest you sitting down and write out all the things you feel make you a great parent. Then write down the things you feel would make you even better at parenting if changed. Once more, DO NOT attempt this in a state of ego or it will backfire and your efforts in this exercise will not work. Take time to meditate on what you write down and let it come from your authentic self. It will help you see yourself from an outside view. You can adjust your life to better your relationships with your children as well as see where you excel in your parenting.

You don't need a person to tell you that you have talent in your job. Your ego is the only thing looking for pats on the back. If you are talented you know it without letting it feed your ego. You can look at the work you do in life and smile with satisfaction instead of feeling you are better than others for it. If you feel there is something else you can do to improve your work, you do just that. Don't find identity in a job, find satisfaction and pride. You don't need to LOOK to others to give you praise to know you did a good job.

Parenting is the same way. You don't need to LOOK for praise in your parenting. You will know you are a good parent when you ARE a good parent and you won't need to gauge it by the child's love. The children who are acquiring you as their step-parent CAN and WILL have feelings that go against how you want things to be. Understand that they are going through a big change and adjustment in their life and need space and time to work through that adjustment just as you may. When it seems they might not give you the attention, appreciation, or love you want, it does not mean you are falling short. Children need to adjust to having a new parental figure just like you need to adjust to becoming a parent. Give them ample time to adjust to this new way of life; it is very important to their acceptance of you as a parent.

You also have to remember (stepfathers especially) that in most of these cases the children are going back and forth from biological parent to step-parent. Having this happen weekly or monthly can be taxing on the child. I have found that time and space is needed here, especially in the beginning of the transformation of the new family. When the child comes home from their other parent's house, it is imperative you give them time to settle and adjust back to your house and environment. As a step-parent, let them come to you. I have found, that not bombarding them with questions or attention, works well in providing the space and time needed for them to adjust back into this household/family. You may give a little attention in saying "hi" or "you missed them" but leave it at that. For them, every time they go through this experience, it is like a reset button taking them back to the feelings of not wanting to betray their biological parent's love. This will take time for them to get through in the beginning, but soon, they will be able to bounce back from these feelings quicker and the time and space they need to adjust will become shorter and shorter. I have seen that the best way for my kids to get through the stress of going back and forth is in this down time given to them.

~The Face of Control~

A Definition of Control: Limits and Restrictions; *"The process of limiting or restricting somebody or something, or the methods used in this."*

One VERY STRONG aspect of the ego is its constant fight for control. Remember the six ways that Diane Zimberoff said the ego seeks to stay alive? "(1) competing; (2) validating its own point of view and invalidating other peoples point of view; (3) making itself right and others wrong; (4) justifying its own behavior; (5) judging the behavior of others; (6) self-aggrandizing."

Break down the actions of the ego and much of it falls under control. Competing gives you a sense of "dominating others", thus it gives the sensation of controlling them or being above them. When you argue to validate your own point at the cost of invalidating another's point of view, you are looking to control the moment, making you right, them wrong, and again gaining control for the ego. It's just another form of controlling other's thoughts, opinions, and actions.

As you can see, the ego is a very control based entity and it thrives on having, or at least perceiving that it has control of its surroundings. If the ego ever feels it has lost its control over someone, something, or some situation, it has a complex it uses to get upset. Then it attacks what it perceives it has lost control over in an effort to regain the control. In a way, you could say, the ego is the ultimate "control freak". If the ego loses the perceived control, then it will act out in many different ways. Whatever way the ego acts out to regain its lost control is the way it perceives would be the easiest, or most efficient way to gain back control. Some will try manipulation, getting angry, making others feel bad for them, while others will be stubborn and unmoving, all in the name of trying to keep the perceived control.

On the other end of the scale, some people love the feeling of being out of control. This frees them for a few moments from the ego, giving them the simulated sensation of being free from ego and complexes, but once the moment is over, they fall right back into an egoic state of thinking. This can be like a drug and in some cases people actually turn to drug use to get the perception of not having control. They will lead a life of chasing the next good rush or feeling of bliss they get from the temporary freedom from ego. This can be a damaging way of life if used to "escape" instead of working to overcome ego.

Others feel a more severe need to control everything around them. These people have very strong egos and most likely an even stronger complex to go along with it.

The ego finds a lot of control in relationships it has throughout life. Friends, family, spouses, co-workers, and even your children are all potential candidates to be controlled. If the ego can't find some aspect of control in the relationship, depending on how strong it is, the ego will back away and avoid egoic contact, or usually attack the subject it feels it has lost control over.

The relationship you have with your children is one of the easiest relationships the ego can fight for or find its control within. That is why your ego gets so upset when it starts to perceive your children are "acting out of control".

If you have ever heard someone tell a parent they need to get their kid under control, you were listening to that person's ego looking down on another for not having control. By voicing its opinion in an obvious situation, it builds itself up to making it clear it would have controlled the situation better.

I was unaware of how the ego thrived so much on feeling in control. My ego would act out at times and later I would wonder why it felt it needed to say, do, or resist something that was not necessary. During a conversation I was having with a friend about egos and their actions in relationships, I picked up on what a controlling entity it really was. To me, it seemed most of the arguments, negatively verbal comments, irrationality with another, anger, or ANY interaction that turns hostile between egos is capable of being narrowed down to one problem. Someone's ego felt it lost some type of control.

When does the ego start to gain a controlling side? A strong and controlling ego will begin at a young age. Looking back at my childhood I realized I started to develop a controlling attitude when I was about ten or so. As I meditated on my younger years to get a grasp of what was going on in my stepson's life, I started to remember feelings of being controlled by my parent's rules and expectations at about the age my son was now. If I had not had such a strong developing ego, then their rules and guidance would not have made me feel like I was being controlled, or under someone else's thumb, so to speak. I would not have had a problem being asked or told to do something, but the fact was I had a strong ego searching for control in life. When it came up against a wall that made it feel like it didn't have control, it would fracture and cause a complex to start growing within.

At times, my stepson would get mad and upset if he was asked to clean his room because, like most kids he didn't favor having to do such chores. It was part of life and important in teaching proper cleanliness, but his ego would fight it. First, he ignored what he was asked to do, then moving into protest he'd sit in his room on the floor not lifting a finger to clean. Sooner or later, it grew into yelling about how he wouldn't do it at all and if we wanted it done, we could do it ourselves. Out of control? At first my own egoic thinking said "yes", but as I started looking at it with a more clear sense of mind, I realized he wasn't. He was just in need of guidance; LOVING guidance.

His ego would be pushing back with strong resistance and when it got to be too much it would bring up a complex. Then his ego would feel it was struggling to keep control. On one occasion his ego started to resist when his mother asked him to clean his room before playing with his friends. It started its resistance by trying to verbally say it wasn't one that would be told what to do. Then it applied resistance by doing the complete opposite and finally it erupted with anger and shouting. Later, after he eventually did clean his room, his ego tried one last time to show it had control. He walked to the corner market after his mother had told him there was no way she would allow it due to how he acted earlier. Nothing like this had ever happened with him. He had always been one to ask and if told "no" he would follow the decisions even if he didn't like it. This time it was his ego acting out as he got older and tried to gather more control over his surroundings.

From the beginning, his mother stayed persistent and told him, "his room will be cleaned", without yelling at him. She was aware it was his ego acting out and he was in a complex of "feeling lesser" from not having control, but did not give it any energy by fighting back or arguing with him. She just stayed calm and let him know it had to be done if he wanted to play with his friends. When he went against his mother's punishment and he knew he was in trouble, she stayed calm. She told him to go in the house and think about what just happened and she would be in to talk to him. Instead of shouting out punishments for his behavior and saying things that gave the ego food for complexes like, "How dare you, you should NEVER go against what I say" or "Who do you think you are acting this way, do you know how mad I am?", she waited until he was calmer to talk to him. Asking him why he felt it was a wrong choice to do what he did and act how he had acted, she let him know that keeping the trust between him and us as parents was essential for his growing up and having privileges. She stayed aware during this entire interaction and gave awareness to his ego and complex. It took time, due to the size of his complex, but the ego and complex finally shrank back. When she told him he was not to hang out with his friends or go anywhere for the next week, he understood. His true self even told his mother he was so sorry he acted that way. And he was downright sincere when he said it. That is the power of not feeding another person's complex and ego. When you give awareness to someone else's complex, the complex has no power to feed from, so it has no choice, but to shrink back and diminish.

In the end, his room got clean. When he had calmed down and talked to his mother about why he acted in such a way, he apologized saying he knew where he had gone wrong, and he loved us. When he said these things you could see it was coming from his heart; not from the ego trying to control/manipulate the situation by saying what the ego thought another wanted to hear. It was truly from his heart, from his higher self.

This awareness his mother had taken on and the loving guidance she was able to bestow was a great lesson for me to observe.

This is just one example of how a child can strive to have control as he or she gets older, but if you are aware of a situation escalating, you can give awareness to your own ego to keep it from feeding fuel to the fire, or feeding the complex of the child.

Not all children will have such a large complex and ego that will struggle for perceived control. Some children may be too young to have developed their ego yet, so it does not affect them so ruthlessly, or create complexes around having a step-parent introduced into their life. Even if the child has a strong ego, as long as you are aware of your ego and work not to let it take over, it will be easier to move through the steps of becoming a family and easier for them to grow close to you. They can form a strong bond right away with you as a parent if they do not feel overtaken or over whelmed by your egoic reactions.

My stepdaughter is a child like this. She was too young to be able to witness and understand the situation that was going on between her mother and her father. She didn't form the strong complexes her brother had to work so hard to overcome. Actually, she seems to be a lot more in touch with the present moment than most, as she has a strong understanding and grasp of reality. At the age of seven she is already very aware of the ego and of being in a complex. She is aware of the reactions that come with both of them, often reminding me that I am not listening to what is really being said when I am in complex. A few moments later I will grasp awareness and see that she was right. I was not listening, or I was not taking time to look outside the box because I was so consumed with negative thinking.

Not to say that she is not an average child, she has her moments of letting ego cloud her thoughts, or letting her emotions run away with her, just as everyone does. As a younger child, my stepdaughter would search out her boundaries of control much the same way her brother or any child would. If asked to do something, like take a bath, or get something from downstairs, there would be every excuse not to do it; she already took a bath the other day, she didn't know how to turn on the bath, or her legs were too tired to get up and go down the stairs. When she realized this was not working she would usually give up the attempted fight for control since her ego did not have as many complexes, she had not had her ego shattered because she had been so young. She was able to skip the birth of the major complexes that were unfortunately haunting her brother.

Sometimes a smaller complex would be at work on her, making her feel pain or frustration from not having control. This would always result in crying and being very dramatic.

As I already mentioned, a lot of this is normal behavior when a child does not want to do something because it is the ego grasping for control. The stronger the ego and the worse the complexes are, the more often they will try to fight for control. Does this mean she was being disobedient when she occasionally acted out? In her mind, she was not trying to be bad. It was the same in my stepson's case. He was not thinking he was in the wrong. If they knew they were in the wrong and still continued to act out, that was when someone was being disobedient. When a child is being overtaken by an ego as it feeds a strong complex, they will act out in a way that seems out of control. Why? It's because their true self does not have control, their ego does. Having their ego in control, they can't perceive they are acting in the wrong way. The ego makes them feel they are being wronged and they need to get back the control in their life in order to be given justice. In reality the true self does not feel the need to be in control. Therefore, there is no need for the true self to fight against life.

Again, not all children are going to have such strong egos, but if they do, then you can understand where they most likely originated. With that understanding it is much easier to give awareness to the ego and complexes that arise. But what about us as adults; what happens when we have strong egos that fight for control?

When an adult has a strong controlling ego, coupled with a complex that is an easy match to feeling hurt over control loss, it can be devastating to a child. Many parents do NOT like to think they have no control over their children, feeling they are not listened to, or obeyed with any sign of resistance, they will argue. Instead of reasoning with, or directing their children, they will argue. Yelling and threaten their children in order to get back the control they perceived they've lost, they do not give awareness and understanding to the child, and by doing this, they will create a controlling ego and possible control freak.

You can NOT give a child's complex and ego awareness or understanding when you are in your own egoic state. What will happen is the two egos will just collide over and over, fighting for the perceived control. Every time you do this, (being the adult) you will overpower the child. This can continually fracture their ego causing the complex to grow every time.

Unfortunately, the child is easy to overpower and becomes the easiest target when an adult ego needs control over something and/or someone. Because of this, you will never be able to raise a child with direction. You and the child will constantly be fighting each other, through your egos, and this gives no direction to the child. Instead they learn nothing but the feeling they will always need to fight for control. Their complex will grow, making them feel negative emotions for not being in control everything around them. So, if you do not give awareness to your ego and complexes, you will not be able to do the same for your children. You will be raising yet another control freak.

I started to realize this when I saw my stepchildren, or at least their egos, starting to follow the lead of my own egoic reaction as it perceived losing the control of something. It was like looking into a mirror of myself when my stepson's ego would struggle for control. I remembered listening to a speech from Deepak Chopra where he mentioned if you want to see what you need to work on in yourself, look to see what bothers you about other people's actions, because others can be a reflection of yourself.

Many people in the spiritual community, not just Deepak, mention that everyone you encounter is a reflection of yourself. I came to learn this is very true when it comes to the children you raise. If you look at children and view their actions and reactions in life, you will have a good idea of how the parents are in their life. That is what I started to see in my own family. The reactions my stepchildren's egos had toward losing what they perceived as control, was the same as my egoic reactions. I was leading by example and in doing so I was showing their egos that it was acceptable to fight for control in any manner. In turn, this leads to pathways in the future you will have to work through and "un-teach". Be aware of your egoic reactions and how it is affected when things SEEM to turn amiss. Be aware of when you start to feel upset and why. Then take the time to meditate and try to understand it. If you want to make it easier to recognize the moments your ego is starting to act up and bring up negative emotions, try keeping a log of what happens.

Here are some steps to help become more aware of how your ego reacts to feeling of losing its perceived control. First, when your ego reacts in a way you later realize was due to feeling out of control, think back to find out when it felt your ego lost that perceived control. Then look to see what steps occurred that lead to your ego trying to get back its control. How did your ego react? Look for the clues that come up to tell you your ego is starting to feel loss of control. Then keep a log of what happened and why. After awhile you will start to see they all have similar actions and reaction and you will notice there are certain clues that can tell you when a situation with your ego may be rising. Then you can give awareness to your ego and what it is feeling, while at the same time giving awareness to the situation and possibly the other individual, which in this case will be your stepchildren. Over time you will be able to stop the egoic reaction and stay aware as you observe your complexes and ego. This will enable you to shrink them down, keep you centered, and in your true authentic self as you give guidance and direction.

Jeremiah D. Kaynor
To Raise A Parent

Chapter 4
Letting Go

One of the hardest things to do is let things go when you have a strong ego that tends to run with negative emotions. Even when you are aware you are in a complex and your ego is taking over the moment, you will find your ego will fight to stay alive. Not wanting to let go of negative thinking, the ego will struggle for control of the moment. You will have the negative commentary running in your head and occasionally you will get a glimpse of awareness that says "You are in complex and it is your ego talking, not you."

Just as fast as that awareness comes, your ego will fight to jump back in and take over making it hard for you to let go of a situation where it feels wronged.

How do you react to someone that offends you? Do you think about it for weeks after the incident? Do you have problems forgiving or getting past what people do to make you feel hurt, angry, or belittled? Most people with strong egos are affected in these ways when people make them feel wronged. My ego loves to hold onto everything that upsets it because it is such a strong ego. This made it so hard to get past any little thing that would happen between me and my family. I would hold onto my exasperation for hours, days, and sometimes weeks when the everyday instances would annoy my ego. Even if I didn't talk about it or act upset to the point of being angry, I would hold it inside and listen to the negative commentary in my head. It affected my interaction with my family in so many negative ways. This state of not letting go of issues is called having a "chip on the shoulder". It leaks out into your speech, body language, and actions.

It reminds me of a children's movie that came out from Pixar called "Meet the Robinsons". It had a character who was a villain and through this villain they gave a lesson on letting go and the effect of having a strong ego. The ego then latches on to being wronged and is not able to let go or move past its offense. The villain was wronged as a little child by another and throughout his whole life he held a grudge against the other child. Consumed by getting even, he missed out on his whole childhood and life. When he is telling his story about how he became the hate filled person he was, the movie shows all the kids being nice to him and wanting to hang out with him. Giving him complements and friendly hellos as they pass him in the school halls, they treated him with kindness. But as an adult he saw everything differently. As he described his childhood he said, "THEY ALL HATED ME!" You could see in the movie, his vision of reality was distorted by his pain body.

It was meant to be humorous but at the same time you could see he was so wrapped up in what happened. His ego was so strong, by holding this grudge he was completely blinded to all that was real. The "chip on his shoulder" stopped him from interacting with other people in a normal way. His ego was so consumed by hate and thoughts of building itself back up by getting even, it destroyed his chances for a happy life. It did not allow him to move on to better things or better thoughts.

This is a strong example and if you watch "Meet the Robinsons", you will see the more overly exaggerated lessons. It will make you laugh at such illogical ways of being, but it does show if your ego won't let go of things that offend it, your view of reality and other people will get distorted. This can block you from enjoying a normal life/relationship with people as it leaks out in every aspect of your life. Ironically you won't even know it's ruining your life.

When you have a strong ego the awareness will last for a few moments, then the ego kicks in and tries to take over again saying, "I don't care. I'm upset and I have the right to be in this emotional state.

How do you start to gain the upper hand on your ego when it has trouble letting go of so many things it encounters? How do you get over the past when it seems every day, something reminds you your ego was wronged, or perceives it was wronged in a situation? How do you hold on to the ever so precious awareness you need in order to overcome and silence the ego when the ego seems stronger than the higher self? How do you start to see the world through the eyes of your true self and not through the distorted vision of the complexes and ego? How do you let go of all the egoic actions and move on to a more pure relationship with your newly found family?

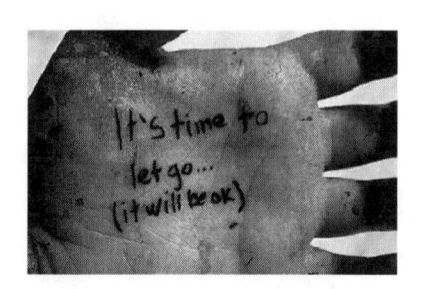

~Letting Go of Identity~

Remember when I was talking to you about finding identity in your life through things that have no REAL meaning to the being you are? Taking on identity through your job, material possessions, friends, the company you keep, and your family, are all common ways to define yourself to other people. Why do you feel the need to define yourself to others? Why define yourself at all? The fact is, you are just you. You don't need to find elevated acceptance from others. You need to know you are exactly who you need to be at this moment; family man, teacher, bread winner, role model and friend. These are all functions you act out in the moment it is needed. They are not a reflection of your inner being because there is nothing short of God's nature that could ever reflect your true self. When you are in your authentic state of mind, you will see, no matter which role you are working with, there is a loving, magical being within. This being is observing, listening, and taking in life a breath of appreciation at a time.

I personally had a lot of trouble letting go of how my ego saw itself, and the identity that it held in life. As I would start letting go of one identity, my ego would try grabbing for another in and effort not to lose itself. The ego needs to identify with anything to have a so called "place in life" and feel it fits in. My ego identified with sports in the beginning of my life. It felt that being a snowboarder, skateboarder and dare devil was how it showed the world who it was. By getting praise for my ability, it felt others could see I was accomplished. But did it show the person inside, the true self? Did it reflect the love and compassion capable of coming from within me? Did it paint a good picture of how amazing my actual existence was?

No! If anything, it was a shallow scratch on the surface of my life. It described nothing about my thoughts on life, my feelings toward the world I coexisted with, or what I wanted from this existence. It was hard to let go of my long standing identity. I would talk about snowboarding and the accomplishments I felt I had done within the sport. I strived to become better than the others that surrounded me and my ego identified with the only thing it could, being above others. This trickled into my daily life and interactions with people. I felt the need to top another person's experience with one I felt was better. My identity was very much wrapped up in being better than others at something and the sports I excelled at were the only thing my ego felt I accomplish with uniqueness.

Looking back, my uniqueness was not from what I had done, but from just existing, period. I wish I had seen that concept much sooner in life.

In finding my identity through my ego, one of the many side effects that came up was how I really hurt my stepson's relationship with me in those moments. He too was someone who loved the sport of skateboarding and in it, found his identity. He was able to identify himself to me through skateboarding and this is where I almost demolished a father/son relationship. I didn't realize my ego was setting the bar so high for him. The egoic shadow I was creating became too hard to stand in and it crushed his spirit.

At first he loved the time we spent together skating, but I started to let my ego overrun the sport and competing aspect of my life. When we were at skate parks together I started to spend less time with him and more time by myself. When my ego started to build itself up through other people at the parks by talking about its accomplishments and identity in skateboarding, he would end up feel shunned or left out. Instead of paying attention to him, I was busy boasting about myself. His abandonment complex was kicking in and being fed by my actions. His ego could not keep up with another ego so big and overpowering. This made him start hating the sport. It got where he never wanted to go skating. My ego had built him another complex wrapped around skateboarding and he would find any reason to be upset with it, even though it was NOT his true self. His was a very bad complex my ego had helped birth. Not that I was the only one responsible for his complex, but my actions did have a BIG part in its growth. My stronghold on my identity in such an egoic "look at me" type of way was driving my stepson and me apart.

One day I realized I was also holding onto the past. I was re-living it over and over as my ego recited its stories to hold onto that specific identity. As I became aware of the now, of the moment life is, and of myself, I started to see I was neglecting reality. I was neglecting being in the present moment and neglecting the person living in this very moment with me. I was not being aware of others around me or the effect I had on them. This is when I became aware of my ego's identity.

I was beginning to see how my ego was viewing itself and how it was holding on to whatever it perceived its identity in. It was not seeing the reactions of others and it was not allowing me to be, or even see my true self. I was completely living in an identity. When I came to understand and was finally aware, I noticed my ego stopped talking nonstop about things it felt defined it. I started to listen more. I started to hear others as they interacted with me. I was observing people and their greatness as beings.

Not that my ego didn't have the urge to speak up and say something about itself when others were telling stories about life, it would always come up and I would have to catch it and come back to being aware of it. As I would gain awareness, instead of getting upset with myself for letting my ego speak out, I would observe it and ask "What just sparked my ego to try and relate or identify with that person's story by relating something from my life?"

It was hard, but the more I became aware of the times it would act out and grasp for identity, the less and less it would come up. I started to really listen to others while engaged in conversation and if my mind or ego would have the urge to speak up and tell a story to identify with the conversation, I would be able to give it awareness and with that I would not let it speak out. It was hard to overcome the urge to tell "My" story, but as I did, I found myself really understanding where the person I was talking to was coming from. In turn, I found it let me be more authentic with myself. Any stories the ego wanted to tell would not be embellished and therefore, I felt more true to myself. Though it was hard to keep in that mindset at all times, it was at least one more step to becoming authentic in life. This was one step closer to the first agreement that Miguel Ruiz spoke about in The Four Agreements: "Be impeccable with your word." As easy as it seems, it's a hard one to apply if you are unaware of your ego in life.

I also started to see myself for who I really was. I began to understand the "I AM" that was life, the true self that was observing everything. It also gave me a chance to start seeing others in my life in a whole new light. I could almost tell when people were talking about their ego's identity because I became aware of how my own was working. I could see right through their ego to their true self. It felt like I was reading between the lines.

One of the most needed changes this awareness caused was with my stepson. The relationship between us changed in such a dramatic way, but at first, I didn't even know it.

Shortly after I had become aware of my ego's identity and started to work on letting it go, my stepson's complex started to subside. His complex surrounding skateboarding started to shrink back and he began wanting to go with me again. His anger towards going to skate parks almost completely burned off and disappeared. When I became aware of my egos identity and the overpowering dominance it had, I started to subside it with that awareness, not letting it be so dominating when it came to skateboarding and other aspects of life. This eased up the pressure had put on my stepson's ego and complex around the sport of skating. Suddenly he felt happy about it again. His ego didn't feel it had to compete with mine and in turn his complex started to shrink.

There was no more tension around skateboarding for him. It was so nice to see this side of him where he was exited to skate again. His attitude change helped me understand when interacting with others in any way, it can be draining and leave a bitter taste in your mouth if you constantly try to build up your ego's identity while casting a shadow over them. There is no need to prove your identity to others in any aspect of life. If you live so much in the identity that the ego carries, you will become competitive and overwhelming to people. This makes them shrink back from you, your ego, and the shadow your identity can cast over them.

The first step in letting go of identity is becoming aware of the identity the ego is taking on. As you do, begin to observe your interactions with others. Listen to your conversational topics when speaking about yourself. Is there a specific subject you replay over and over to people when you are talking about yourself? When people are in conversation with you, do you tend to try and make a specific subject about your life fit into the conversation? What about when your mind is daydreaming? Is there a specific job or action you reflect on that makes you feel superior to others?

Not that it is wrong to dream or imagine what it would be like to succeed in life through actions, or even reflect on past accomplishments, but you don't want to let your ego hold on to certain actions just to make it feel better than others. Again, if you can start to observe your thought patterns and conversation patterns when thinking or speaking about yourself, you can begin to pick up on what your ego finds identity in.

When you find out what those identities are, you can start to let them go and begin to understand they really don't carry any true meaning in life. Be aware of the difference between the function or role you are playing out when finding identity with something. Ask yourself, "Am I any less of a person if I was to lose this identity? If it was taken away or lost, what is left of me? Do I define myself through this identity?"

Meditating on these questions in regard to these identities your ego is holding onto can help you start separating the true self from the function.

It was very hard for me to come to terms with the fact the identity my ego had held onto all those years was not who I was. I still catch myself occasionally beginning to talk or think about it like it was a long lost friend. It's because my ego feels a strong need to have a place in life, to have an identity that sets it out from others. Unfortunately, it completely pulls me out of being in the moment.

Now, when people ask me what I "do in life", or anything to that affect, I try not to stick to a repetitive character or identity in my answers. I try to speak in the present moment of my life as much as I can. "I write, I invest, I paint, I have my family to take care of," and so on and so on. As I speak of these things, I keep in mind that the "I" being talked about is not who I am and I'm merely referring to the roles I have to play out in life to go from point A to point B.

Keeping this in mind will help stop your ego from overwhelming others and give you a closer look into your true self. Letting go of identity and not letting your ego pull you back into it is a hard thing to do, but when you do, your relationships become more authentic. When you begin to get a better grasp of self, those others around you pick up on this and their attitude begins to change toward you. They will feel more comfortable and closer to you. For stepchildren, this is a grand key to building a relationship with them. It allows them to feel close and open with you instead of feeling you are a competing ego. All because you separated your egoic identity from your true self and stayed more present in the moment, you're allowing your children to enjoy the real you. Echart Tolle made it simple when he said in reference to identity, "'I' embodies the primordial error, a misperception of who you are, an illusory sense of identity. This is the ego." What you feel your identity is, is your misperception of yourself.

Echart Tolle points out, the word "I" and other words pertaining to self are used widely in an egoic reference to identity. Not that the use of the word "I" always pertains to the ego's view of itself and its identity, but it is essential to letting go of egoic identity to be able to distinguish the difference in the use of the word, when used by ego, or used by the true self, while not being held by the egoic idea of who you are. Tolle later states that, "If you can recognize this illusion, it dissolves. Its recognition is also its ending. Its survival depends on your mistaking it for reality."

So as you become aware of your egoic identity, it is the beginning of the end for it. This is the start of letting go of identity. The more you are aware of it, the faster it dissolves. Over time you will realize you are letting go of the identity the ego used to view as itself. For my ego, this came over a span of around 2 years because of the strength my ego had and still strives to hold. Slowly I realized it was not me and I had no need to portray myself as a function or role, therefore giving the ego identity. My mind still tries to pull back to it now and then, but as the moments pass, it becomes less and less of an instinctual action to fall back into ego.

Jeremiah D. Kaynor
To Raise A Parent

~Letting Go of the Past~

On the Top 20 Things listed as "WHAT OPRAH KNOWS FOR SURE" is number three; "Whatever someone did to you in the past has no power over the present. Only you give it power."

Ah the past. It's an amazing illusion we hold onto. I learned a lot about living in the moment and letting the past be the past. I found there are two sides to letting go of the past, the intellectual and the emotional. The first time I really understood the idea of the past was while I was at work.

Truth be told, I was wrapped up in complex for most of the morning over something that had happened, not in MY past but in Dasha's past. It was years before she and I had even met and really had nothing to do with me. To top it off, my perception of what happened and why it happened was completely clouded by complex. It was just a detail of a story I had been told.

She had told me that the boyfriend she had through college was a very physically abusive person. The things he had done to her were horrific and she was too scared to leave in fear he would take things too far. This is, from what I have learned, an unfortunate outcome of many abusive relationships. The abuser has so much control over the abused that the abused is terrified to leave or upset the person for fear of bringing on more vicious acts.

I, on the other hand, at the time, had no clue how a relationship could ever get to a point where someone was afraid of leaving because my mind had never observed that in life. In turn, my ego grabbed that and used it to feed a complex within my mind. My complex was feeling I could not be loved as much as others in life, or in this moment, "more than she loved him". Do you see a reoccurring theme in my egoic thinking behavior?

I battle with that one complex a lot, but the more I am aware of it, the more it dissipates, letting me see reality clearly. In regard to my misperception of the past, I was getting worked up and letting my mind ponder and soak in the thoughts of Dasha's past relationship. Thinking to myself, that the only REAL reason she stayed with him was due to her immense love for him, how could I ever compete with a love that could make someone endure such terrible treatment? Coupled with the instinctual want for the person you love, to only have been with and loved you, can keep a complex rolling in negative energy.

As you can see, my egoic complex was very good at distorting reality. My whole morning at work was taken up by my thoughts fermenting in such a hurtful, unhealthy, thinking pattern and all brought on by egoic thinking. I was wrapped up in the past, fogged by a misperception, and letting the only thing that mattered get affected, the present moment. As soon as I became aware of this, the ego started to fade a little, and the negative thinking I had running through my head started to battle with awareness. My mind was telling me, "You are in a state of egoic thinking and it is not necessary. It's just the past, you didn't even know her then and there has to be a better way of looking at this."

With that classified, my ego would jump in and try to take over with "It doesn't matter. She stayed with him because he was better than you could ever be. You have a right to be hurt and upset. She just wants me to know she loved someone else so much she wouldn't leave him for any reason."

Truth is, she never said anything of the sort. My mind only heard one thing (I was "with" a really abusive person in college) and from that point on, I made my own conclusions about how things were. It was amazing when I became aware of what was outside the confining box of my egoic thinking. My entire mind had been hanging on the fact she was with someone else. It was something my ego didn't want to hear, so it made up this big story wrapped around the fact she was with someone else, just to feed a complex. That's it. That's all that happened and I lost a good chunk of a perfectly good day to a past that had nothing to do with me. It wasn't even real, according to how I was seeing it. If I had stayed in the present moment and not let my ego run away into a fictional past, I could have saved myself from a lot of stress and anguish.

This was just the first step in letting go of the past. I didn't know it, but the awareness was starting to corrode the ego little by little. I had heard teachers say being aware was a key point in shrinking back the ego, but I had no idea how eye opening it could be until I sat there really observing my mind play out these little battles. The first time I became aware, I almost wanted to laugh at myself because it seemed ridiculous how my ego was fighting so hard to stay alive and in control. It was almost like my inner being was shaking its head at someone throwing a tantrum within my own thoughts. In a new relationship there is always a lot of past you will need to move through, and some people have a "don't ask, don't tell" attitude when it comes to the past of someone they are choosing to be with. It may *seem* like the smart thing to do when there is no reason to bring up "dirty laundry", but it can still seep out one way or another. When you are not totally open and honest with your partner, it can create a gap that keeps you from being as close and loving as possible.

Why don't people want to know about their loved one's past and why does it cause problems when it's brought up?

The past, for some magical reason, can make a person, or at least their ego, feel jealous when they actually had nothing to do with it at any given time. The only time the past affects you is in the now or in the present moment because you are reliving it in your own mind *now*. Allowing yourself to stress out, get angry, or feel hurt by something in the past, you are *allowing* it to affect your present moment. So it's our ego inquiring about past relationships, looking to excavate fuel to feed your complexes. If the ego didn't gain from keeping the past alive, then it would just be another story in a conversation with little or no meaning. Why? Because the true self does not live in past or future, it is only in the present moment. The ego is the only thing that lives through the past and future. Any reaction to the past from the true self would be more of an impassive reaction. There would be no reason to be bothered because the only thing that is, is the present moment.

On the other side of the coin, the only one telling stories (instead of inquiring about them) of the past is the ego. Searching for a way to build itself up, the ego will dig up little known facts and memories for reasons to keeping itself alive. Have you ever noticed when you become very aware of the present moment, ego is not there? It does not exist in the "Now". There is no incessant need to talk about the past or itself (the ego) in accordance with the past.

Echart Tolle brings out a good point in "The Power of Now" when he mentions the past is happening now. You are thinking of it NOW, reliving it in your mind at the very moment you are in. Hence, the past does not exist besides in the present moment. And it's only if you bring it into that moment. So you could say that people really do have the problem of living in the past because they allow their present moment awareness to be taken away by a moment that no longer exists. This makes the past the present because the only way the past can stay alive is when it is in the present moment.

This can affect a step-parent's relationship very harshly if he or she is not aware of it. In these relationships, you have a lot of past experiences your ego can use to feed complexes and in turn, blind you to what's real in the moment you are in.

When involved in a relationship where there are children not biologically yours, you may have many inward battles over trying not to letting the past interfere with the now. It is harder to let go of the past when your ego is faced with the so called past of your partner on a daily basis. Having to work with the biological parent in co-parenting the children can bring up many complex based thoughts that can cloud your vision to what is really happening in the present. It's a reminder that there was once a relationship between the one you love and another. For many people, it is something they don't want to face and it can be hard for them to accept. Or I should say, it's something hard for the ego to accept.

Your mind can dwell for long periods of time in the past without allowing others in on your mental situation. The only problem with this is, it takes you out of the present moment, feeds the ego and complex, lets things fester in your mind, and allows your emotions to build up until something pops.

I had such a hard time letting go of the past sitting in front of me with my two stepchildren. It wasn't even a past I had anything to do with. Any time something would come up between my ego and Dasha's ego, my mind or ego would start a rolling commentary of, "Why don't you just get back together with your ex?! That's the best thing for you and the children. You don't need me!"

Sometimes those thoughts would come out verbally if I was not careful. Looking back, I think it was a way the ego was trying to get one of two things. One, reassurance that she would never leave, and two, it was trying to feed the complex, so it would stay in the emotional state of feeling bad for itself.

If you have a stronger ego, such an ego will distort reality and weigh you down by a past with no more existence than what you give it. You have no control over past experiences and because you don't, the ego feels threatened by what it doesn't like. It took a while for me to get this, but when I finally became aware of the way my ego would cling to the past, it finally had no bearing on the present moment. It now had less effect on my mind. It felt as if I was just listening to another story when it was brought up.

I was not always able to keep the awareness needed to let go of the past, but over time letting go was easier. If I felt any tense or negative emotion come up because of a story I was hearing, the emotion would disperse quickly and the story would be just that. A story.

The only thing from the past that should have any influence on someone's relationship in the present moment is reoccurring problems with drug, alcohol abuse, anger issues, abusiveness, and so on. Those are the types of things you should concern yourself with. The rest of the past we hold onto is an absent and distorted memory which holds no jurisdiction or power over the present moment.

Now that we have gone over the intellectual side of it, let's go over the emotional side of letting go. This is a second step to letting go of the past. The emotions that come up when the ego is confronted by the past can be very overwhelming. Anger, sadness, pain, and frustration, can all have an effect on you when dealing with the past. If you only deal with the intellectual knowledge of how your ego works and try to get a handle on your harmful thinking by just being aware, I found you will only get so far. You too, will find that your emotions will end up a jumble of frustration.

First, you will become aware you are feeling upset by a past experience, and then you will get frustrated with yourself for feeling that way. You will feel like you should have a handle on your emotions, but, you don't need to control them. It is just another way your ego is trying to slip in and get you thinking negatively. Be aware of the ego and the emotion.

When you start to feel hurt, upset, threatened, sad, or any other emotions that may come up when confronted by your partners past, just be with those emotions, don't act on them. Let them run through without giving them any energy. It's a complex that has come up in the present, and by not letting it have a reactive charge to build off of, it cannot stay active for long. (We will be covering how to observe or be aware of your emotions a little more in depth in Chapter Six.)

Become aware of what complexes your ego is using to make you feel bad about the past and realize when you are in complex surrounding a past experience, the ego is using the past to feed complexes. At this time, make sure you give uncharged awareness to your emotions or complexes that do arise. The more you go through this process, the less it will affect the ego because the ego will not be able to draw any negative action from the experience. In this way you are letting go of the past. So why does our ego react so negatively toward our partner's past in the first place? It's something our ego doesn't have, have had, or will ever have control over.

That leads us into letting go of the need to control.

~Letting Go of Control~

As I said earlier, the ego is a control freak. Needing to have a grasp of control in some aspect of almost everything it is involved with. If you break down a lot of issues in any relationship you will find it boils down to feeling a lack of control over the other individual.

When building a parental relationship with a stepchild you will come up against the wall of control in many different ways. Your ego will strive and struggle to get a handle on things instead of walking gently through whatever issue is presented at the time.

To let go of the instinct to control every aspect of your life can feel like going against a river, but when done, it releases so much of the ego. This gives you a clearer look at what is happening in front of you. To let go of control is to let go of ego.

Yes, it is easier said than done. It is like having someone tell you to let go of the steering wheel of your car while driving on the freeway. You have the instinct to grab it back the instant you start to move out of your lane of comfort. The perception of control gives the ego comfort and therein feels like it's a "must have" in life. If the ego didn't have control, what would it be? It would just be a shadow of a being. It would lose all sense of identity.

For a long time I didn't realize a lot of frustration in my relationship with Dasha and the kids stemmed from feeling I was not in control of certain aspects of my life. I would get irritated with so many situations, while in turn, brought stress into my life and theirs. If the kids would not listen, I would get frustrated or "pissed off", as I referred to it. I would raise my voice when telling them how I felt things had to be, instead of keeping a calm mind about it and working with them to teach and instruct. It felt like I had to "keep them in line".

But that was my ego being damaged by feeling a loss of control. It stopped me from working with them on what I saw as a human level. Instead, it felt more like trying to keep a leash on an animal. This was because my ego was fighting to have control.

One night Dasha told me about a realization she had about her ego and how it was striving to have control over her son. She said when he would get a poor grade on a school assignment it made her feel upset and her ego would kick into full gear. She would get frustrated with him and at times be completely over taken by ego. Why? It was because her ego felt it was a reflection on her when her son didn't do his best. Instead of taking into account he was getting an A+ on a lot of his work, she was focused on the times he got an F here or there. Looking through the eyes of ego, his F's gave her a sense of no control over her world. It took a few times of her feeling very upset and frustrated with him for her to recognize what it was stemming from.

What was the solution? Instead of trying to control him by forcing him to sit down right away and do homework, we gave him an atmosphere that was easier for him to work on his own. We gave him time to relax and be a kid after school, then gave him a scheduled time to work on his school work in the evening. We would not hover over him or be there to keep him focused. The result was, he stepped up and took the responsibility to get it done. He didn't fight it because his young ego was not feeling it was being controlled.

You have to recognize when your ego is working to control others. With this recognition, you can look at situations differently, work on letting go of the perceived control, and then start finding better solutions to life's obstacles.

I still work on letting go of the controlling need my ego tries to hold onto. I have found in many cases, I have to go through the situation before I see what my ego was doing. This gives me insight for the next time so I will be aware of the egoic control, and work on looking at things from a better point of view. It allows me the chance to see it from everyone's perspective, not just mine, and I am no longer trying to control the circumstances.

I know I say that often, but I can't say it enough. Awareness is the key to letting go of ego. It dissolves it and soon there is nothing left but residual toxins that are far easier to deal with.

~Seeing what's Real~

By now you should have a pretty good idea of how your ego works. You should start to recognize the way your mind reacts to situations and see what complexes you have. This awareness will help you work through the complexes.

I have talked a lot about how the mind/ego can cloud reality, but the good news is, the more you face and understand the ego, the more you will recognize it WHEN it comes up and not an hour later. This will stop you from acting/reacting through ego, then regretting your words or actions due to being in a complex. You will be able to recognize the signs of emotion that indicate a complex is coming up, along with your specific thought patterns that indicate the ego is up and attempting to control the moment.

As stated earlier, when you are in complex and your ego is in a heightened state, you are blinded from seeing the true situation.

I found that my ego will either try to compete, defend its perceived self, i.e. "justifying its own behavior", or the big one, "making itself right and others wrong". Whenever I was in complex or my ego was in a defensive mode it would typically be acting out one of these three reactions. At some points I was mulishly blind to the other side of the situation, therefore blind to any other perspective, but my egos.

Once I was out of complex, or not in a complete state of ego, people would be able to talk to me instead of having me argue my point of view. The kid's or Dasha's side of the situation would be more understanding.

The times I would feel the emotions of hurt or frustration from something said or done would be overwhelming, because I resided in ego so much. As soon as I was "over it" and out of ego or complex, I could see there had been no reason at all to feel offended. Essentially, I would see what was real.

I mentioned once before about Greg Dambour, the man that gave spiritual tours of the vortexes in Sedona, Arizona. Remember what he said about being in a low mood, when feeling bad, or offensive about a situation? He said "Stop and ask yourself: 'How can I look at this a different way?'"

The moment you come into clarity after your mind has finally let go of ego or complex is when you are able to see the answer to the question. The trick to seeing what is real is to get a grasp on the ability to see your complexes or the ego coming up as they are starting to awaken in the moment. You may feel a tightening of the chest, or a rush of energy flowing through your skin as if your emotions are seeping out. There are many signs you can become aware of when your ego arises. First if you observe what you felt physically and emotionally, you can bring your attention to them. You don't want to act on them, just feel them, and observe them without judgment. When becoming aware of your ego and complexes you will notice you do this quite often.

In a sense you are learning how your mind works. As you are able to recognize the egoic states arise, you will be able to ask yourself the question Greg Dambour presented. "How can I look at this in a different way?" Instead of reacting, you will be able to stop and see the situation from every angle, and have a more understanding point of view.

I can't tell you how many times it took me to get to the point where I was able to resist reacting to a situation. Sometimes, my ego was so active I would be aware I was in complex and I would ask that question within, only to have my ego struggle to gain control and answer back "There is no other way to look at it. I'm upset with just cause".

But the farther I got with awareness, the more I was able to stop reacting. This would give me a chance to consider the situation at hand.

I would go even farther into the question and ask myself "Is there really a reason for me to have these emotions that are arising or is it just my ego trying to feed a complex?" After being able to begin seeing things from a different perspective I was able to move through the moment without having a complete egoic reaction to it.

Hard? Yes, at first it is very hard, especially when your ego is strong and stubborn. But when you are able to interact with your new family, who tend to bring up egoic complexes, without speaking from your ego, everything runs smoother. You will have understanding compassion for the situation, and you are able to let go to see what is really going on with your stepchildren and your partner. Eventually you will be able to interact on a mature level with the other bio-parent to work together raising the children in their present environment. You will see the only thing that is real is the fact the young child or children are dependent on the parents (YOU, your partner, and the other bio-parent) to raise, protect, and guide them in life. This is the most important reality you must be aware of at any given moment.

Letting go of unnecessary egoic reactions and seeing what is real in the moment, can and will bring you into a closer relationship with your new family. You will see there is nothing beneficial in being attached to an identity, control, or a past experience that is worth the torment it can bring you or your children in a step-parent/stepchild relationship.

Chapter 5
Breaking the Walls Of Pre-conceived Concepts

As I mentioned earlier, a per-conceived concept is an aspect of thinking that limits us from seeing life for what it really is and can be. After moving through ego, it becomes easier to recognize these pre-conceived concepts and change your point of view from assumed, to understanding and openness. This will bring you even farther into seeing what is real.

There are many pre-conceived concepts deeply rooted in our minds as we grow through life. There are assumptions made based on observing situations. Your mind does not take into account that there is not one situation identical to another. Not one moment is exactly the same as the last. Everything that happens cannot be compared to another's experience. Why? Because the thought patterns and egoic reactions differ from person to person. Some egos are stronger than others. Everyone has a different level of perception and life's circumstances will always differ from the slightest to the largest dissimilarity and cannot be approached in the same way.

Jeremiah D. Kaynor
To Raise A Parent

~What We Are Taught~

Life gives us so many misperceptions as we walk through it. Mostly it is someone else's point of view that gets passed on to you like they had it passed on to them. Much of what we are taught in life is someone else's personal opinion.

A good example would be my understanding of politics, or the lack of. When I try and join in on conversations, I know I am severely risking being a little off because I don't get information for any unbiased source. Everything I know about politics is from other people's viewpoints. Do you think I can have an accurate understanding of government and politics from other's personal views? That would be a big "NO" because there are so many different ideas and opinions out there! Many of us have understandings we perceive as written in stone when we learned them from another's opinions or perceptions. It can be difficult to move through and weed out the opinion from fact when there are so many different views.

As we grow up we are taught many different pre-conceived concepts surrounding step-parents, stepchildren, and the whole family institution. Children learn the "Wicked Stepmother" concept from a young age and that paints a picture of how step-parents should and will be. I am sure you have seen a movie where the new step-parent comes into the family and right away tries to come between the children and parent. There is also the concept that stepchildren will try and ruin your life and get in the way of you being happy with their bio-parent. All of this is well represented in media and Hollywood. It seems to make for a good story in people's eyes and then they come away with the negative thoughts about stepfamilies.

As you grow in life you seem to think you know just what is real due to ideas being planted in your mind. These give birth to pre-conceived concepts. The truth is, everyone has a different perception of life. Not one person's ego is exactly the same as another. They all exist at different levels. Not one moment is a repeat of an already experienced moment. Not one person's emotion emulates another's because everyone feels their emotions in their own way. Just as everyone is unique, so is every situation. Even the situations in this book that I am sharing with you, can and will differ from yours.

My life as a stepfather is not a template for you to follow, but more of an example for you to look at, to get an idea of what is going on with your emotions and mind. A sign saying "Stop, look within. It's imperative!" Once you start down the path to become a step-parent, you are the one who can take the message I am trying to pass on and apply it to your specific family in the way you can use it to have more insight into yourself and the ones you love.

Jeremiah D. Kaynor
To Raise A Parent

~What We Observe~

A pre-conceived concept can also be a perception that you gather from quick assumption due to experience. Many of us do this as we hurry through life and do not pay attention to our surroundings like we should. I have been a prime example of this. All my life I could remember parents, friends, and now my wife telling me to slow down with life. Not only was it something that others could recognize, but the universe would always put something in front of me to let me know to "slow down and enjoy the view". I would be completely oblivious to things that were happening because I was trying to rush through everything I did. For that, I would make many assumptions that were not correct. In my mind I would "assume" that a situation was the way it was because I would make judgment on what was happening before seeing it from all angles. My mind would take a moment and place judgment on it without observing it to its fullest.

It would be like a person walked past another without ever talking to them, and decided they already knew what kind of personality they had. They made this judgment from the clothes the person was wearing, the hairstyle he/she had, and the smile or lack of one they might have displayed. By that, they assumed the person was or was not someone they could ever relate to.

Was this a fair judgment? No, it was the "judging a book by its cover" bit. As you do this, you build pre-conceived concepts throughout your mind of how the world is, and you don't give it a chance to show you what is really going on.

I found myself working through so many different pre-conceived concepts after I met my family and started to settle in as a stepfather. These concepts were misleading notions I was oblivious to in life until I started to live them. I entered into moments thinking I already knew the outcome or the "reality" of the situation, but why did I suddenly become aware of them now? What blocked me from seeing the truth and reality behind life this entire time? What opened up my mind at this stage in life?

~Opening Up the Mind~

When I started to become aware of the ego, my mind started to become clearer. I began to be aware of things that I either took for granted or thought I already understood. So what changed? I started to live less and less in an egoic state of mind. The more aware I became of my own mind, world started to change.

When you are not clouded by ego you are able to see the world through the eyes of the true self. It observes life in a different way, not judging a moment, a situation, a person, or an idea.

Remember when I told you about the time I could not find my toothbrush due to thinking it should be in a standing position like my wife's? My mind, after seeing hers in a standing position, had assumed mine should be doing the same. From the moment I assumed that, I got more and more frustrated with the fact I could not find it. The farther into the frustration I got, the less likely I was able to see it. The instant it was pointed out to me, my mind stopped its negative irritation. The mind had clarity and the reality became apparent. It was not that I had to be taken out of ego to see what was right in front of my eyes, but I had to resist moving into the moment with a pre-judging thought. Right when I did see the toothbrush, my ego let go of the irritation, my mind opened, and I realized what had happened. Suddenly I understood the assumption and understood the idea of why my mind held onto that assumption after it was made. Because I was in an egoic state as my mind got frustrated with the situation, I was not able to be open to any other ideas.

I found with step-parenting, you come into this realization quite a bit the farther you get into the relationship with your new family. The thoughts and assumptions that have been planted by society and other's assumed ideas will block a lot of growth between you and the children in the beginning, if left unnoticed. They can be devastating by blinding you to the opportunities life is giving you to grow closer to your stepchildren. But if you recognize the existence of the pre-conceived concepts and become aware of their affect on your thinking, it helps open up the doorway to thinking outside the box. The easiest first step to this is becoming aware of the ego and complexes. Even if you don't have the ego all the way diminished (Monks and Yogis work life times to get to that point), it gives some stepping blocks to opening up your mind to reality. You will be able to recognize pre-conceived concepts much easier and from there, begin to stop them from controlling your outlook on life. As soon as your outlook changes you start to see life for what it really is. Your mind will open up to every possibility instead of just one, and you will be able to react or make judgment from a clear state of mind.

Chapter 6
Becoming Aware

I know I have said a lot about being aware of ego, complex, and pre-conceived concepts, but I can't reiterate it enough. Like I said in the beginning, the information in this book is vital to a relationship that will need insight to help it grow into a strong bond of love and trust. So again we talk about awareness. This IS the key to starting the gain of insight from your true self, away from the ego and complexes. You might still be wondering how, just being aware of the problem makes it diminish? How do you become aware of something that you seemingly have lived with your whole life and not known about? Well the easiest way I can teach is by example. I could talk forever about meditation, contemplation, observing the emotions, and so on, but I think I have already made that clear. So observe my path and example of becoming aware in the following situation.

Jeremiah D. Kaynor
To Raise A Parent

~I Was Unaware and Blind~

As already stated, a big problem in a relationship with a new family is when your ego seeks to build itself up by outside forces, such as accomplishments and approval from others. You can very easily lose sight of what is happening right in front of you when your ego is focused on what others think about YOU, or even if it is striving to look better than others. You can miss seeing the effect it has on the ones that are closest to you. You are not doing it consciously, but you are building a gap between you and others around you.

I had this problem when it came to the egoic image I held about myself. The ego used snowboarding and skateboarding to build itself up. I was so wrapped up in how others viewed me and trying to improve my skill in the sport, I completely ignored what was going on with my new growing family. My now stepson, as you remember, was very much into the same sport I was involved with. He too accelerated in the sport as he was sponsored for his ability. *At first*, it was something that brought us together, giving us a common bond. If you have a common interest with the stepchildren, this can be used as a great tool as long as you realize that it will be special to them. Used in the right way will bring you closer, but taken for granted, it can hinder the relationship, as you will see with us.

Like I said, we had this common bond. We both loved skateboarding and did it as much as we could together as a family. It brought us together at first, but then slowly unraveled. He started to hate skateboarding, not wanting to go and getting upset at the mention of the idea. I know it was a little hard on him because he moved up a bracket in his competitions from beginner to intermediate. The level of skateboarding was harder and he was used to always winning first place in competitions, so I chalked it up to what I thought was poor sportsmanship when it came to competing.

It was easy to place blame on his sportsmanship because it was his nature to take it really hard when he wasn't the best in a sport. He has a very competitive nature, just like I do, if unchecked. Many of us have the drive to strive for excellence and he has a drive in him that will get him a long way in life if used properly. But when it came to his anger and complex wrapped around a sport that he loved so much, I didn't get how he could be so upset for not being the best. That was where I fell short of seeing reality. WAY

SHORT! That was only a small fracture in his ego when it came to skateboarding.

It was easy for my ego to look at the situation and shake my head thinking "Here is a kid that needs some serious work on good sportsmanship". When Ryan was in complex and angry, my ego would look down on him for it. At times, his complex would feed off my ego and say mean things about me in front of people we knew from skateboarding. My ego would spark up and get offended, there by feeding his complex by expressing its frustration (through body language or comments). It was an ongoing battle. I felt there was nothing I could do to fix the situation. I was not looking at myself to see what I was doing to add to the complex this young boy was going through. I was failing to be the step-parent he needed. So what was REALLY going on here? Why had our common bond been broken, causing a division between us? What was I missing? Why did he have so many negative emotions wrapped up in something he had once loved?

I would like to say I figured it out before it got too hard on Ryan and me, but I didn't. It took some time and frustration on both our parts. It was frustration that didn't need to happen. If I had been aware of what was really going on, I could have eased the pain his complex was putting him through, or helped him to move through it completely.

The problem was, I was so engulfed with myself and how I was being perceived by others, I consequently missed the clues that were telling me what was happening to my soon to be stepson. For him, skateboarding was the bond between us. US!!! But right before I met Dasha, his father had taken him skateboarding every now and then, to be supportive of Ryan. That was a big deal to Ryan, but I did not recognize or know that when I came into the picture. I came in at a level of riding that was intimidating as far as skateboarding had gone. To some, it would have made them feel a little overwhelmed, and unfortunately, with our unconscious egos at work, I fear that is what happened with Ryan's father. He backed away from supporting Ryan in his skateboarding and that was where a little fracture started within Ryan's ego. He felt he was losing his dad's support, maybe even feeling a little abandoned, so at this time he latched on to me. A crutch if you may. I did not know this at the time so I was not able to balance things out between Ryan, his dad, and me. This is something that could have been worked out within a short time, but then, I made it worse.

As Ryan and I would skateboard together we spent more and more time bonding. Unfortunately, with an ego so used to finding acceptance, approval, and being marveled at by others, it was hard at work trying to gain what it needed to build itself up.

As we were visiting skate parks, we were seeing the normal kids and people we knew from the world of skateboarding. I started to spend a little more time with other people as they would build up my ego. I would be talking to them about tricks that they or I were working on, or just skate with the little older crowd that was at the parks. I started to spend less time with Ryan and more time "showing off" while giving attention to people I thought I needed approval from. I was ignoring the only people and the one person that really counted in my life at that moment. Hence, he started to feel abandoned again in his skateboarding by a father figure.

Feeling he had to compete for my attention with riders that were on a higher level, he would get angry with people he had never met. Due to his mixture of wanting to strive to be the best, and feeling he was losing my attention to these more experienced people, he felt threatened.

It opened up a big abandonment wound for him. Soon he even started to get upset if his friends talked to kids he didn't know. He felt threatened by their presence and perceive he was being betrayed, or abandoned, if attention was not given exclusively to him. An abandonment complex came up within him fast. It was one he had gotten from his earlier experience with his father while they were going through hard times. It had been opened even deeper by my unconscious egotistic actions. It was a big complex and I didn't see that it may have sprouted from his father. I was feeding it and giving it the power it needed to grow to full strength just because I was acting in unconsciousness. In turn, he quit skateboarding and took up basketball instead. This was a huge step away from his talent in skateboarding.

~Opening My Eyes and Mind~

It was quite a while before I became aware of what was really going on with Ryan. About a year later I was sitting down with a family counselor talking about some of the struggles I was having with Ryan and how I didn't know what was going on with him. I told the counselor "I don't know what his problem is."

I was frustrated and worn out from butting heads with him and having him so angry at me all the time for what seemed like no reason. I told her I didn't know why he hated skateboarding with such a passion now.

She looked at me and said "It has a lot to do with you."

It reminded me of a quote I had read from Rumi saying "People of the world don't look at themselves, and so they blame one another."

I had not seen it within me because I was not looking at myself.

Feeling he needed approval from a father figure, and perceiving he lost it around skateboarding, he attached it to basketball, consciously knowing it was more his biological fathers style, thus feeling there would be more approval in it.

As I started looking back on the times there were major problems, I was shocked to realize I was completely and unconsciously opening up the wounds that were putting him in complex. By paying less and less attention to him, while involved with the social group I had known my whole life, in his mind, I was just another male figure leaving him behind, therefore feeding his abandonment complex.

I never wanted to be that kind of person to him, so from that point on, I decided I was going to be supportive of him in everything he did. Coupled with his dad coaching the basketball team and me attending games to cheer him on, he started to get support and approval from both directions. His ego still had the striving need to win at everything and be better than everyone, but in the face of losing, we made sure to show him he was still supported, and we were proud of him.

After his attempt to take on basketball, he got excited about football. This was at the beginning of his mother's and my marriage, so it was a highly volatile period for his ego, and all the emotions surrounding his mother getting married again. I wanted to give him the attention and support he needed while being aware of everything going on with his emotions, not turning a blind eye to his feelings like before.

When it came time for football season, we also started him back into a little bit of skateboarding to help him see he could do both sports if he wanted to. I made sure to be supportive of his football. His dad would help coach the team, while I helped Ryan personally at home. I worked one on one with him catching, kicking, throwing, and just giving him the attention he needed as a stepson.

It was as if there was a shift within him. All that was needed was some awareness given to his ego and my ego, his complex and the complexes it would bring up within me. Once I was able to be aware of this, I was able to shape-shift my actions and reactions from an egoic form to a more loving and supportive form. When his complexes would arise I would respond less and less from ego and instead more and more from a loving understanding view.

He started to enjoy skateboarding again. He ended up meeting a large group of friends from around our new neighborhood who were his age and also liked to skateboard. They would come over and skate on the half pipe that I had built for him. It turned out that one of his skateboarding friends was also on his football team. This showed him that he could do both sports at the same time and there was no need to only focus on one sport or hobby. He was able to start releasing the complex that was entangled with skateboarding because I became aware of my ego, and worked on not letting it search out its own recognition and identity. This made it easier for him and his complex. I finally saw it wasn't all about me anymore. He was my son and I needed to shine my own light on him instead of trying to put it on myself. I started to see things from a different perspective. A perspective of a stepfather and not from my ego's perceived view of life. I was able to give him what he needed; love and support.

Even though my ego would arise now and then, I strived to stay aware of it. I would say I was aware of it only about 5% of the time, but that was what it took to start the shift in our lives as stepfather and stepson. That began a massive shift in our relationship.

The "Change the World Project" web page says about awareness: "Global awareness helps us evolve as a human race. When there is a need, we can systematically analyze the need or problem and then design solutions."

This is also true on a smaller scale, such as personal awareness. It gives you the power to "analyze the need or problem and then design solutions" for your family. It's a gift from the heart to yourself and to all around you.

Jeremiah D. Kaynor
To Raise A Parent

~Striving To Stay In the Present Moment~

It is harder to stay aware than it sounds. It is no wonder that monks, shaman, spiritual gurus and teachers around the world strive for it their whole life. You may, at times, feel as if it is completely out of reach for you. I know I have come up against that wall myself. The thing to remember is, it only takes a small amount of awareness to start the ball rolling in your life and in the lives of others around you.

I found that staying in the moment comes and goes. It is difficult to hold onto present moment awareness at all times when we live such chaotic lives. Many of the spiritual teachers give advice on meditations to bring you into present moment awareness. The best technique I have found, that seems to be universal, is concentrating on your breathing. Feel your lungs fill with air as you inhale, then releasing tension as you exhale. Do the best you can to let go of all thought, then, come back to your center.

Now, when tension in my new family starts to get elevated for any reason, we have all agreed to call a "pause". Anyone in the family can do it if they feel there is a need to stop and work their way back to their center, or away from ego or complex. If someone is under attack by another's ego, they also can call the pause. Sometimes, it may need to be called two or three times before the other person or persons honor the pause. But all are in agreement it should be honored, and the person is given space and time to get out of complex. It has been a real asset to us in helping the family members get out of complex and let the ego subside. I, for one, have an ego that sometimes needs to hear the pause called a few times before my awareness kicks in. At that moment, I will sometimes leave the room when a pause is called and go lay down until the tension has left my body.

We are also able to call a pause on ourselves if need be. When one is feeling they are moving into complex, or if their ego is getting agitated, they can call a pause if someone tries to interact at that moment. This is a good exercise to help as you become aware of ego and complex; spotting them as they arise, so not to act on them. My wife has mastered this one and can spot her complexes a mile away. This gives you time to settle back and not let the moment be frazzled from ego and complex.

While taking the time to work on subsiding the ego, you can use this opportunity to observe the emotions your body is feeling. Get familiar with the physical reaction your body has as it responds to your heightened egoic state.

~Observing Your Emotions~

When you are at the point you are able to observe from your higher self; to see, feel, and search through the emotions that come with complex and ego, there are two ways I have found to work through them.

One; as you meditate on your complexes, you will feel the strong emotions come up inside. You can track the feelings and emotions your complex is bringing throughout your life, and pinpoint where the complexes were first introduced into your thinking pattern. This will help you work on letting go of the hurt, offense, or loss which started the complex in the first place. This will give you some insight into your complexes. With insight you can start to shrink the complexes with even quicker awareness as they arise. You'll understand why those feelings are coming up and realize they are being used to twist the view of the present moment.

Two; when not able to pinpoint the beginning of a complex, you can at least meditate on the emotions, giving them awareness and understanding. I have observed that it feels the same as giving understanding to a small child who is hurt and crying. If a child falls and scraps their knee, you don't yell at them for falling. You pick them up and give them love, making everything all better. Giving understanding to your emotions as they come up works in the same way. When observing them from the true self, be understanding to the emotions as if you were to be understanding to a hurt child. This will slowly diminish the complex because you are not feeding it with negative reaction.

To become more aware of the emotions you are feeling when in the complex, observe the emotion as it arises in the moment. What does it do to your body? Do you feel a tightening in muscles or a heaviness of the chest? Do you have a nervous reaction such as popping joints, popping your neck, stretching or clenching your jaw? Such things can indicate your body is in an emotional state of distress. Can you feel what it is doing to your face? I know it may sound like a funny question, but take the time to feel the emotion as it runs through your facial muscles. Your body reacts physically to emotion, and can be a good compass for when you are starting to come into complex.

When you get familiar with the physical feeling starting to arise, you can use that awareness to work on not reacting on those emotions. This will keep you from feeding the complex, thus giving it energy. It will start to lose effectiveness and slowly diminish.

You can also track the emotion back to its origin, and find out what may have started the complex in the first place. When you get a chance, meditate and try to remember the last time you felt that same emotion. Do you remember what triggered it? What is the earliest you can recall having that emotion? Does it remind you of a particular event when the complex and emotion came up? What similarities are there in the event that happened then and now?

By spelunking into your emotions, ego, and complexes, you will be able to do much deeper work within yourself. Being able to weed out the ego from the higher self will allow you to "analyze the need or problem and then design solutions" with sound judgment and love.

Sometimes you may need outside help to be able to understand what triggers bring you into complex. Again, complex is a state of complication. Sometimes for a person to be able to sort out all the mess that one's ego can make. It can be even harder when placed within a new stepfamily and trying to decipher what is real and what isn't.

I heard a man on the radio once say that he and his family go to family counseling on a bi-weekly basis. The man on the show was giving advice to a gentleman about sending his daughter to military school, due to her getting into so much trouble. The talk show host asked him if he had ever been to counseling with his daughter and family. The man said he had never thought about it. In reply, the talk show host said, and I quote, "I think every family should take time to have counseling. It does not mean you are messed up in any way, shape, or form. Bringing a professional into the mix, even if it is once a month, helps the whole family work on deep seated issues that you normally wouldn't ever address. The issues seep out in ways you could not imagine. Even I go once a month on my own because it is easier to do deeper work when you have someone there that can guide you through the psyche. If you are serious about helping your daughter, get counseling for her, you, AND the whole family."

I had to admit, he was right about having outside help from a person that could guide you and your family through the inner workings of the mind. It can be done without any outside help, but the truth of the matter is, it really speeds up the process. It's like going to school to learn about yourself. Like I said before, it is a gift from the heart to yourself and to all others around you.

~ Giving Children Guidance from Your Higher Self~

Guidance is an essential gift you give your children. They need it. They crave it. They depend on their parents to give it. You, as a step-parent, will be a major player in this role bestowed upon only the worthy. I have to admit, there have been times I should have given guidance to my stepchildren, but backed down because I let my ego and complex take over, making me feel I was not the person my stepchildren wanted parenting them.

Looking back, even if I was to give the guidance, it would have been coming from a prejudiced, egoic state of mind, not from my higher self. It doesn't come from the clearest view of life and understanding. At the time, if I had worked through the emotions that were coming up and gotten myself out of a state of complex, I could have given the guidance my stepchildren needed.

If you take the time to move through your complex and get out of the state of ego, the guidance in life given from the true self, when you are in your center, will be the inspiring, life changing guidance the child needs.

The thing is, when you have a child in an egoic state of mind, and you are joining his or hers egoic acting out, by butting heads and arguing YOUR point of view, the child will stay in that egoic state until it is forced to leave your presence. It will go off in a huff (or you will) and stew on all that it feels has just wronged it. But when approached in a state of mind not controlled by your ego and complexes, you will be able to talk to them calmly. Even if their ego is kicking up, showing its anger, pain, frustration, or sadness, you will be able to talk from your center, allowing you to reason with them on a calm level. By doing this, you will see their ego, whatever state it is in, diminish. Depending on the severity of the egoic state, it may be quickly or it may be a little while. Either way, the guidance given from your state of mind, from the higher self, will have a long, lasting repercussion down the road, if not right away.

This is what your child needs. They need you. Not your ego or complex. They need the real you. This is how they grow in a healthy manner.

Chapter 7
Parenting Partnership
And
Tips to Bring Ease on
The Relationships

The parenting partnership, between you and the ex-spouse, is imperative and hopefully you will be working with someone who wants to be involved with their children's raising and well-being. If not, then the sole responsibility falls on you to be the father or mother that is missing in the child's life. This may make it easier, but in reality, the best thing for the children, is to see that their other bio-parent has an interest in their lives and loves them. If not, it will bring up some deep seeded issues later on in life. I think we can all agree, if any of us were, or are in the position of having parents living in different households; we would want to know they both love you and want you in their life.

HELLO
my name is

Co-Parenting Meetups...
Coming to a Location
Near You!

~A Co-Parenting Schedule~

It took me a while to warm up to working with the kids' dad as a co-parent in raising them. It went against everything my ego stood for, and I had to be able to let go of so much and move past emotions. The important thing in this part of the picture is not your personal feelings. It is the well-being and proper raising of the children. When I did get through that part of my ego, it ended up making everything so much smoother. Their father and I were able to talk about what needed to be done with homework, what events the children had planned to attend (birthdays, field trips, sports, and so on), and if there were changes needing attention. Setting consistent standards from one household to the other is important.

The one thing children need is consistency. If they are not allowed to have certain eating habits at one household, it needs to apply to the other household as well. If not, you will come up against a wall every time and make it harder on one parent or the other.

This also goes for other daily life routines such as bed times, the importance of homework, and so on. If you are not able to communicate well with the other parent, there will be a gap in the parenting. This will make it harder on the children when it comes to their environmental re-adjustment every time they move from one bio-parent to the other. You, as a step-parent, need to make sure you are working along with the other parent and not against them.

If they are allowed to do something at your house and not allowed to do it at their dad's, they will expect him to bend on his standards and give him grief for not allowing it. This puts pressure on him and the kids. There needs to be this consistency for the children in their lives to run smoother and easier while moving back and forth from household to household.

You will also find that the children will test the waters by trying to pit parents against parents. There have been a number of times that my kids have tried to tell me their dad had let them do something I did not feel comfortable being allowed. After asking their dad, I would find out, it was not true. They were just trying to test the boundaries like I talked about in Chapter Two.

Without the open communication, it would be hard to know the direction to move when it came to guiding the children. The easiest one for the children to try and manipulate is the homework aspect. Saying it was done with the other parent when it wasn't, is a common one I am sure you will come across.

When you get down to it, the key element you must have, is clear and open communication between households, as every parent works together as a team to raise the children you all love.

If you are having problems working together with children's biological parent, I suggest you do some work and try to resolve the issues wrapped up in this part of everyone's parenting. The sooner you are able to move past your egoic mindset and diminish any complexes that may be interfering with the co-parenting, the better for you, for the children, and for the other parent. Like I said, the important thing is not your personal feelings or egoic thinking, but it is the well-being and proper raising of the children.

You are partners in raising the children. It does not have to go past that relationship. You want to have the understanding that you both have one thing in common, the well-being of your children.

This is the responsibility that you take on as a parent. Making sure they are loved, raised properly, and given guidance when needed.

In certain parts of the globe, when a child is born into a tribe, the whole tribe takes on responsibility to raise the child. Not just the parents are there for the children but everyone. Why should it be any different with the ones who are involved with your children? If you keep in mind the goals and objectives you and the other parent have when it comes to the children you both love, you will be able to work with ease to raise your little ones.

Jeremiah D. Kaynor
To Raise A Parent

~The Ease of Boundaries~

Another way of making it easier on the children is by giving separation to the two families. I know this may seem hard, but it is part of giving boundaries to the relationships. Dasha and her ex had to sit through counseling to find where they needed to set boundaries in their lives. This was an important step for the children, pertaining to their and understanding of life as it would be for them. They needed to know that mom and dad's lives were separate and the only connection they needed was to raise the children. To make it easier on the kids, they decided it would be best to make it less stressful to transfer from mom's home to dad's home. The first thing they did was eliminate the whole packing process. The kid's dad bought them clothing they would keep at his house so there was no packing and unpacking every weekend. This took away one stress from the transition. Second, he set them up with their own room in his house. This created a home away from home instead of a "spending the night somewhere" type of experience. The next step was to limit the mixing of the two parent's lives. Understanding that everyone's situation is different, as a family, this is what we found worked for us.

Their dad used to walking into our home when he came to get the children. Now, he waits outside for them to come out. In return, we would have them ready to go when he pulls up. In the beginning of establishing our family, we felt that, because Dasha never went into his home and with him always walking into ours, it was overstepping bounds and privacy, and it also showed the kids it was JUST mom putting up a wall between their father and mother. This made it harder for them to be accepting of Mom's new life without Dad. Now that he has a significant other in his life, they have been able to adjust quickly and easily to their Dad's life change and the comfort level has loosened up.

We also split up the birthday parties so both bio-parents threw their own party for each child. This was nice for the kids too. Now they had two birthday parties each, and got a lot more presents, which they love. It helps to be positive about the fact they have two separate families. Let them know they have twice the love and twice the people to protect and guide them through life.

Before we started setting boundaries, they didn't understand why Dad could be so close to Mom's home life without being part of it. This can go both ways. If the mother is intruding in the father's life, it will confuse the children in the same way, not letting them move on, or adjust in a healthy and natural way.

When we set those boundaries, the children adjusted in such an amazing way. The mood that they experienced while in the transition phase changed dramatically. In the beginning, it is important for you all to set boundaries. This will make it so there is not such a grey area to the children when it comes to the different families. Once the separate families are established, things will get easier as the co-parenting becomes more comfortable and the interaction will be relaxed.

Remember when I talked about giving them time and space as it is needed when they first come home? This is your boundary for them. I mentioned that when the child comes home from the other parent's house, it is imperative that you give them time. Time to settle and adjust back to this house and environment. As the stepparent, let them come to you, and do not bombard them with questions or attention like I mentioned in Chapter 3.

Saying "Hi" or that "you missed them" is fine, but leave it at that. Remember, for them, every time they go through this experience, it is like a reset button, taking them back to the feelings of not wanting to betray their biological parent's love.

There is also a wound here that opens every time they have to go through this. It takes time, but it does heal with your support and understanding. In the beginning this will take them longer to get through, but as time goes on, they will be able to bounce back from these feelings quicker. Soon, the time and space they need to adjust back will become shorter and shorter.

The best way I have seen for my kids to get through the stress of going back and forth, is this down time given to them.

The other person you need to avoid working against is your spouse. I know you think there is no way this could be an issue, but you have to understand, there is an established way of parenting here, that, in most cases, has been in effect for years before you came into the picture. You of course will be part of the parenting more and more as time goes on, but you have to know, the children have already gotten used to a certain way of adult guidance. The best way to ease into it is to sit and talk with your partner about how your parenting is going to be approached with their child or children.

Many people adopt their ways of raising a child from how they themselves were raised by their parents. This might conflict with the strategy the bio-parent might have. Being open to discussion is a key to not having conflict in the raising and guidance of the children.

~Avoid Guidance From the Ego ~

There will be times your ego will want to take control of a situation it feels should be parented a certain way, but you must differentiate the difference of egoic guidance and guidance from your true self. Being aware of when the ego comes into the picture with its negative thinking, will help you avoid giving guidance or punishment in an egoic state.

You can tell ego is aroused by a situation if you feel irritated and personally offended by what the children have done or are doing. This has been a struggle for me. It's hard, but I work to resist reverting back into an egoic state of mind when I work with the kids and their actions have been less than acceptable. My egoic thinking is strong and triggered easily, so I have to work twice as much to stay aware of what is going on in my mind and emotions.

There are many times I have acted from ego, yelled out of frustration, or gotten upset saying, "What's wrong with you? Why would you do or say such a thing?", or my egos favorite one, "I'm sick and tired of your actions."

Jeremiah D. Kaynor
To Raise A Parent

Am I the one that is "sick and tired" or is it my ego being rubbed the wrong way? I feel when I am within my center, or my true self, I'm not easily annoyed by my kids' actions and behavior. At the same time, I tend to be able to talk to them and bring their energy level down to a point where they can understand how their actions are not quite nice, acceptable, or right.

I have learned, and I'm still learning, that the best way of teaching your children is by example. People hear of this their whole lives, but I don't think they really get it until they have children. Just now, I'm realizing how much of a mirror the children are in a parent's life. If you don't quarrel with your spouse (their parent), the bickering between them and their siblings lessens. They start treating others the way they see you treat people. Working with the parent in an easy manner, shows the children that working as a team will greatly increase their ability to do the same with others in life, including you, as well as their peers.

When you teach from a state outside of ego and complex, there is only one outcome. The lesson will be heard. They may have to be reminded of it from time to time, but the fact is, they hear it from you much more clearly. When you are in an egoic state and getting frustrated with them, they tune you out.

~Working With Your Partner~

Make sure to keep open communication between you and your partner on how they want their children to be approached or punishment assigned, when they have acted out and done wrong. If you are both able to stay on the same page when it comes to raising the children it will be easier on you and the whole family. Everything will be consistent and run smoother.

You also need to make sure you don't go against or undermine the other parent. This can cause gaps and walls within your relationship, as well as you and the children.

When I get into an irritable egoic state I tend to stumble into this one. I think the worst scene is when I ask the kids to do something and I get that push or resistance from them. Right when their mom joins in and also asks them to comply, I tend to fall into the victim roll and say "Never mind, I will do it myself."

I go off thinking, "How can they be so lazy?" and "They can't do anything I ask of them because they don't see me as a parent". Do you see where my ego likes to go with that one? It's incredible that I don't see it at the time. Right at that moment I have taken away their mother's teaching powers as well as my own. I undermine their mother when I let my ego react like that and in doing so give them no chance at learning.

Avoiding this one is key. Undermining the other parent can give an incredibly bad example to the children and cause so much damage in the long run.

Again, it is best to be open and discuss the plan of how to raise the children and stick to that plan. Consistency is such a huge key factor here, I can't say it enough. There have been many times when "battles" were won because we stayed firm and consistent with things we expected in our household.

For example, when the kids hated to eat healthy foods and complained about it every day, Dasha stayed consistent. Over time Gabby and Ryan started to ask for foods that were healthy. They would pass up candy for fruits and drink water instead of begging for soda pop. They started WANTING to be healthy and to eat healthy foods.

There were times along the lines of eating healthy when I would think I was giving them a treat and would buy them pop or candy knowing their mother was not approving. Every time it came to the same end result. She would ask me "Why would you do that, you know I don't want our kids eating unhealthy junk?"

She was trying to teach them the benefits of eating right, and I was undermining her efforts in order to make the kids love me more in that moment. The kids would get a stomach ache or headache from putting foods into their body when it was learning to reject unhealthy foods. Again, I would understand that, by thinking I was going to be the "fun" parent who let them overindulge in treats that were not good for them, I was not helping in the long run.

I have had this issue with my ego for some time, where it tries to gain the love of others by giving in unnecessary amounts. This is an egoic way of thinking that cannot only undermine parenting, but other areas as well. I still work on giving awareness to it every day. I advise you to find the points where your ego looks to work its way out and give it special attention. Your relationship will be much easier when you work on the areas where your ego and complexes are the strongest.

Jeremiah D. Kaynor
To Raise A Parent

Chapter 8
Making Mistakes
And
Recovering From the Fall

But what if you do fall to the clutches of ego and make parenting or family mistakes? What are the consequences within a stepfamily? What do you do to fix them or recover from them?

I made mention of one of my ego's major faults at the end of the last chapter: My ego's incessant need to look for approval from others.

In the beginning of my relationship with my family, I worked through what I thought was a MAJOR egoic state of being, but it ended up sneaking back into my life through a different route.

I had worked very hard and I thought that I was done with that egoic thinking of looking for the acceptance of others in the world, but I was wrong. If it couldn't get what it wanted through the outer world of people, it decided to re-manifest itself into my family. This came about by giving too freely to my family. It may not seem like such a bad thing, but when you have a stepfamily you are ALWAYS looking to for approval, it can run amuck in your life.

To get the perceived approval and acceptance from my stepchildren, I got into the mode of not saying "no". I even let it happen with Dasha. Whatever the kids asked for I would get it for them. If Dasha mentioned it would be nice to eventually get something, I would go out and buy it for her without consulting her about it. Even though it was slowly draining us financially, I would still spend money on things that were really not necessary.

I am sure you can see where this is heading.

Knowing we couldn't always afford everything they wanted, I would not discuss the matter with Dasha. My ego knew she would rather not have things if we couldn't afford them at the time, but I would just go out and get whatever was asked for. My ego was trying to fill the high it got from getting its so called approval from my family. Not seeing how they already loved and accepted me, I continued this destructive path of over spending. It eventually got us into a financial hole. I was doing everything I could to give them what my ego thought they wanted because my ego felt it was the only way to gain love from them.

I really never saw that part of my ego coming back into play because I had thought I was over that chapter. It just goes to prove there is no letting down your guard when it comes to your egoic thinking. Having awareness should be a constant effort on your part. If not, then the ego will act out in other ways where you don't give attention.

As it was, I ended up putting unnecessary stress on my family. Financial issues are the number one cause of stress in a family. When the parents are stressed out about things, the children pick up on that energy. Therefore, it brings low moods to the household and pulls on everyone involved.

I was very shocked when realized my ego was still active in the area of looking for acceptance. I had to seriously look into why I had been blinded to my ego's actions this time around. It was a massive lack of awareness on my part. What caused it?

The fact I had already dealt with this aspect of my ego, gave me false security. I let down my guard of awareness and when I did, the ego acted out. In this second round my family was the target because they were the easiest ones for it to gain approval from.

It's a stepfamily, so of course, your ego is going to be looking for acceptance. It couldn't be a more perfect feeding ground.

Unfortunately, in a stepfamily, there is a lot at risk when mistakes are made. You are supposed to be the healer, not the one to hinder. Due to their situation, these children and your partner already have a life prone to stress. You do not need to be adding to it. You are the one there to save and protect them, to make things better, and relieve the stress of a single parent's life.

So the lesson I have taken away from this situation was, I always need to stay aware of the ego. Just because you get through an aspect of the ego does not mean it will give up and not try to come at life from a different angle. It will. So it is imperative you always strive to keep awareness in life. If you don't, then there is no doubt your ego will get the best of you. The last thing you want to do is guide a stepfamily through ego.

If you do fall victim to strong egoic actions and your family is affected by it, you need to become aware and turn it around right away. Do not let go of that awareness. Do not take the ego for granted. Strive to be aware of what type of action your ego had used to feed its complexes or fulfill its needs. If it is a big problem, focus on working through it before any more damage is done to your world and to your family.

Chapter 9
The Archetype
~
The Step-Parent That Will Change the World

You are a guide and guardian to these children now that you have made the choice to take on the step-parent role. You never want to lose sight of that. These are children who crave your attention as well as your guidance. They need to be shown the path of life and given a hand to hold, as they practice before they are let off into the world.

As a parent you are the one responsible for their life as it grows. Therefore, you want to make sure you are taking the responsibility seriously. I can't tell you how many times I lost sight of that in the first couple of years. It is a big job to take on, but an honor that will never be matched in life again.

You are taking on a role of father/mother, friend, guardian, and savior. The gift you have to give has the potential to be life changing. Don't ever lose sight of that. The moment you do, you will slip back a few steps on the path you have started.

Unfortunately, this world has become a place where families are broken up and lives are shattered on a daily basis. We need to start taking the right steps and making the right choices to heal the world that has had so many parts of it crumble.

As you walk onto the path of step-parenting, keep in mind that you are the hope and the light for these children you are bringing into your world. You are melding two worlds into each other and that takes more effort than you could ever envision. The road to success as a step-parent is the road that will take you to the unlimited possibilities of love, happiness, and beauty. Don't let ego get in the way of making it there. The only thing ego can do is erode the relationship before it has a chance to blossom.

Look at the child or children you have joined in life. They are your future and you are theirs. They can save you just as much as you can save them. They will teach you more about yourself than you could ever learn anywhere else in life. In return you can heal their world, as long as you don't let yourself be guided by ego. In time, you will look back and realize you created miracles. You will see the children you have are God's miracles given back to you.

Teach them, protect them, love them, guide them, and cherish them.

Thoughts to Live By

When you feel frustrated and don't know what to do as a parent, clear your mind, become still in your thoughts and actions. The answer will come.

Jeremiah D. Kaynor
To Raise A Parent

When having a troublesome time with the children,

Just remember…

This too shall pass

Every day brings a new beginning and another chance to start fresh. Don't hold onto yesterday. Live the now.

Jeremiah D. Kaynor
To Raise A Parent

Being a parent is the hardest job you will ever take on. But it is also the most rewarding job in the world. You will remember that every time you look at your child from a distance and your true self gives a smile of love.

Jeremiah D. Kaynor
To Raise A Parent

When you first learn to love yourself, you will be able to offer true love back to the world.

If something is failing in the relationship with your children, it is the universe giving you a sign that you need to change what you are doing.

Remember always,

You have the power to heal a child's world.

In doing so,

You are a reflection of God.

Recommended Reading

Miguel Ruiz: *The Four Agreements*

Eckhart Tolle: *The Power of Now*

Eckhart Tolle: *A New Earth*

Abraham Hicks: *Getting into the Vortex*

Abraham Hicks: *Who You Really Are*

Deepak Chopra: *The Seven Spiritual Laws for Parents*

Dr Wayne W Dyer: *Change Your Thoughts – Change Your Life*

Diane Zimberoff: *Breaking Free from the Victim Trap*

Diane Zimberoff: *Longing for Belonging*

Greg Dambour: *The Woodstock Bridge*

11:11

Jeremiah D. Kaynor
To Raise A Parent

It's worth every step.

Made in the USA
San Bernardino, CA
18 December 2013